The Doom Game Editor

Joe Pantuso

WILEY

John Wiley & Sons, Inc.
New York • Chichester • Brisbane • Toronto • Singapore

To my wife

Acknowledgments:

I owe a debt of gratitude to all the people who have purchased the Doom Editor: without you I could not justify all the hard work that has gone into it. Thanks also to Rob McKnight for his help in compiling the CD-ROM; Mark Gresbach for letting me use Ledges; and Mike Helm for what seemed like endless testing and suggestions. And of course, thanks to id Software for their enlightened approach to software distribution and for making a game we all love to play.

Publisher: K. Schowalter
Senior Editor: Tim Ryan
Managing Editor: Frank Grazioli
Text Design & Composition: Pronto Design & Production, Inc.

This text is printed on acid-free paper.

Library of Congress Cataloging-in-Publication Data:

Pantuso, Joe.
    The DOOM game editor / Joe Pantuso
          p.   cm.
    Includes index.
    ISBN 0 471-12128-2 (acid-free)

Printed in the United States of America
10 9 8 7 6 5 4 2 1

Contents

Chapter 3	Beginning to Build Your Own Levels	45

CONTENTS

Introduction

Welcome to the brave new world of Doom editing. Now that you have torn Hell down, you can rebuild it from your own dark imagination. This book will guide you through technical and creative issues, and show you step by step what to do to create your own Doom levels—even how to create an entirely new game.

Creating Doom add-ons is at least as much fun as playing Doom was in the first place. You can build a replica of your office, your house, or your school and walk through it in Doom. Determined Doom Fanatics can even create new monsters, modify old ones, or imbed real-life friends and enemies right into their new worlds.

Who's This Book For?

Anyone who plays Doom or is curious about Doom and wants to learn more about what makes it tick will enjoy this book. Creating new Doom levels, graphics, and sound is great fun and well within the reach of everyone.

While you might feel like a programmer and an artist as you make changes to Doom, you don't need to be either. No traditional programming or artistic skills are needed to use any of the tools.

What Do You Need?

If you already have any version of Microsoft Windows and Registered Doom or Doom II, this book contains

everything you need to create new levels, graphics, and sound for your Doom games. The included CD contains a powerful level editor, graphics and sound utilities, and example levels. Using these tools, this book will take you to places in Doom you never imagined could exist.

To make use of this book, you must have either Registered Doom or Doom II, purchased from a store or by mail order. Registered Doom has all three episodes in it. If you have never seen a *Cacodemon* or used a *teleporter,* you may not have the right version of Doom.

 What's Inside?

In the back of the book you will find a CD-ROM. This CD contains many useful tools for creating your own Doom levels, in addition to more than 1,000 new Doom levels. Each utility contains its own complete documentation, besides being discussed within this book. See Appendix A for more information on the CD-ROM.

The book's chapters cover the following:

1. **History of Doom and the Doom Editor**—The history of id and Doom, and of the RG Doom editor used in this book. Learn more about the game we love and the people who created it.

2. **Master WAD and PWAD Structure**—The technical details of the data structures used by Doom.

3. **Beginning to Build Your Own Levels**—Level Design 101 gets you going with the basics of level creation,

including placing new rooms, doors, pools, and columns.

4. **Testing Your Level**—How to save your creations and load them into Doom. Troubleshooting information will help you avoid common pitfalls—or climb out of them.

5. **Finishing Your Level**—Level Design 102 continues the lessons as you create a teleporter and a lift and learn what makes special structures in Doom work.

6. **Designing Levels for DeathMatch**—Advanced Level Design takes you to the edge, creating things never before seen in Doom. You will learn how to make splattering your friends more fun.

At the end of this book you will find four useful appendixes that contain reference information.

Appendix A lists all the software that comes with the book, and tells you how to install it so that you can begin building your own Doom levels. You will also find information on getting updates and using shareware. Appendix B is a quick reference guide to the Doom Editor's commands and menu options. Appendix C gives suggestions for naming your new Doom levels, and Appendix D discusses the Doom Sound Editor.

Getting Started the Quick Way

If you want to get your feet wet, bloody, and raw right away, start with Level Design 101. Turn to Chapter 3 and the section "How to Build Your First Level" and install the editor. Then jump to Chapter 4, and you will be walking around rooms you created in 10 minutes. Go!

 # Advanced Users

If you already have experience editing Doom levels, this book will help you polish your technique, and can serve as a valuable reference. The Line Specials list in Chapter 5 will save you time finding that perfect trick. Chapter 6 will show you techniques never before found in Doom, and Chapter 2 will help you get that extra ounce out of Doom.

CHAPTER 1

History of Doom and the Doom Editor

History of id and Doom

id emerged from simple beginnings, and even with two huge hits on its hands and more to come, it still keeps things simple. Started on a $2,000 check, id has grown into a company that brings in more than $100,000 a week, but the folks at id still make sure they have fun.

The Early Days

It all started at a company called Softdisk in Shreveport, Louisiana. The founders of id, John Carmack, John Romero, and Adrian Carmack (who is not related to either John), worked on projects at Softdisk. The approach of Softdisk was to create games on a monthly basis—a sort of digital sweatshop.

Meanwhile, Scott Miller, the president of Apogee Software Limited, saw some of the games that were being created at Softdisk and decided he wanted them for his own company. Miller wanted these guys to work for him. With no other way to get through to them, Miller began sending them fan mail, and asked that they write him back.

The fan mail was read, tacked up on a wall, and promptly forgotten. It was not until months later, when Romero was reading an article in a game magazine, that he realized most of his fan mail had the same address on it—that of Scott Miller at Apogee.

Miller gave Romero and Carmack a check for $2,000, and they started work on *Commander Keen*, quitting their jobs at Softdisk and forming id Software, in Madison, Wisconsin. (The name "id" comes from

Freudian psychology. The id is the unconscious part of a person that drives a person toward pleasure; it follows the pleasure principle.) The agreement was for id to create the software and Apogee to distribute it, splitting the profits. *Commander Keen* was a huge success, setting records for shareware distribution of a game.

Now that it had a source of income, id took on some more people. Reaching back to their Softdisk roots, the partners hired artist Kevin Cloud, business manager Jay Wilbur, and the creative Tom Hall. Unable or unwilling to tolerate the Wisconsin winters, the id staff looked for a more pleasant location. They picked Texas to be closer to Apogee, and decided on Mesquite because it had a lake. The plan was to buy a house on the lake, but it wasn't until after they had moved there that they discovered the lake had no private frontage. Some days are like that.

Wolf 3D

The original Castle Wolfenstein was a popular game in the days when the Apple II was cool. Players saw a view from above their characters and walked them through a maze of Nazis, trying to escape.

John Carmack improved upon the game by adding a 3D engine, and id gave birth to Wolfenstein 3D. It was a great success. Game play was smooth and fun, and the 3D was much better than anything that had been done on a PC to date.

Wolfenstein 3D grabbed more attention than any shareware game before it, smashing the Commander Keen sales record more than fivefold. Wolf 3D could be found on nearly every BBS in the country and, soon, in the world. The only flaw in this success story was that the game was banned in Germany because it contained Nazi symbols and the likeness of Hitler, but that didn't stop thousands of people there from downloading it anyway.

Then a strange thing happened. People were so involved with and excited by Wolf 3D that they began to tinker with it. First, people figured out how to extract the structure data so that they could print maps and find all the secret doors. Bitmap pictures of maps began appearing on BBSs. Then the editors themselves appeared on BBSs. Soon people were using the editors to make changes to their games or to cheat. A few enterprising people created entirely new levels and uploaded them to BBSs for others to try.

As great as the Wolf 3D engine was, John Carmack was unhappy with it even before it was shipped. He knew that if he only had more time, a much better engine was possible.

They're Green and Pissed

Wolf 3D had been developed in only six months, and only a month of that time had been devoted to designing the engine. While the rest of the crew worked on the graphics, sound, and maps for Wolf 3D, John Carmack went back to work. During this time, he developed a new, more advanced engine that was to be used by Raven software to develop a game called Shadowcaster.

With that experience under his belt and even better ideas in mind, he began work on the engine for what id was then calling *They're Green and Pissed*. The new engine allowed for different heights of floors and ceilings, changes in lighting, and texture-mapped floors and ceilings. Walls were no longer confined to an "8 foot thick" grid; they could be positioned at any angle.

It was during the design stage of the game's development that a conflict arose within id Software. Creative director Tom Hall got too creative, insisting that a detailed and consistent story line be given to the game. John Romero and John Carmack wanted the game to be simple. This wise choice to avoid the complexity that is often given to computer games allowed Doom to be focused on game play, but also meant that id and Hall parted ways. Hall went to work for Apogee as a project manager.

Some features that were planned for the game had to be cut because they were too time consuming to develop or slowed down the game too much. For example, with light sourcing and light diminishing, rooms lit up when a weapon fired or a barrel exploded. Such effects had to be created by hand through careful editing. The original BFG firing animation had to be scaled down because the graphics and sound were so complex that they brought the game to a standstill.

id had also wanted to have changing textures that could, for example, show information terminals, writing on the wall, or damage to the wall. In this way a "clean" wall could become marred with a shotgun blast. This, too, was dropped.

Some things had to be dropped because they would have increased the size of the program beyond what was practical. Two such features were a display of damage to players and an indication of what weapon a player was holding during multiplayer play. Just to show a single undamaged player with one weapon requires over 50 separate images, since images are needed for eight different viewing angles, and additional images for each angle are needed to show animation when the player is moving, firing, falling dead, and exploding. These images take up a total of 150k, and if graphics were used to indicate which weapon a player was holding, this total would increase to more than a megabyte. If three different states of damage were shown, the storage would balloon to three megabytes, and so on.

After many changes and months of hard but creative work, Doom was unleashed on a mostly unsuspecting public. You know the rest.

History of the RG Doom Editor

The Renegade Graphics Doom Editor came into existence because I didn't feel like doing the work I should have been doing.

The release of Doom was anticipated widely. A FAQ about the game was around months before the game was ever released. I waited anxiously for the shareware version and downloaded it within hours after it became available. Twenty-four hours later I had finished playing Episode One.

Credit card clenched in my caffeine-palsied hand, I called the 800 number for the distributor and ordered the registered version. When it arrived, my schedule from then on was shot—all work went out the window for several days. I had seldom been so drawn into a game, certainly never an action game.

In January of '94, having played the game to death, I started thinking about modifying it. I was well aware of all the different programs Wolf 3D had spawned and knew that modifications were both possible and desirable. I remembered reading that id intended to fully support people who wanted to create editors and so on, so I attempted to contact them.

id had apparently decided not to release editing information for several months after the release of the game. Since I didn't want to wait untold months, I set off on my own. At this point no one had published any sort of information about the structure of the data files Doom was using, so I started exploring.

I was thrilled and relieved to discover, within minutes of starting, that there was a directory at the end of the IWAD file, apparently an index to the data within the file. I quickly confirmed this by seeing how blocks of obviously different data started at offsets pointed to by the directory.

The directory was pleasantly easy to read as well. The names were all in plain English. Once I located the entries E1M1 and THINGS, I was well on my way. Noting how long the data that made up the THINGS for the first level was, I went into Doom and painstakingly counted all the things so I could figure out how many bytes each one consisted of. Unfortunately, this proved to be a waste of time—not having played any network games yet, I failed to realize there were objects on the level that I could not see, and so my count was wrong.

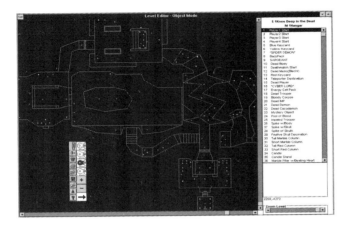

FIGURE 1.1

The first Renegade Graphics Doom Editor (Version 0.9a).

I started to change numbers in the THINGS data more or less at random, using a hex editor. By observing the effects of my changes, I slowly but surely found the meaning of everything. I discovered the proper number of bytes that made up eachTHING; once I got the trick of it, the pattern was obvious. The process was fun, sort of a game in itself (if you like that sort of thing).

I wrote a simple program to extract the THINGS data and display dots at their relative locations. Jackpot! I could recognize the placement of the things just fine.

I next looked at the VERTEXES information. Since I knew what a vertex was, it was very simple to decipher the data: simply a list of x,y pairs. When I plotted these points on the map with the things, I knew I had hit the jackpot again; I could see the shape of the map.

It took a full day to decipher all that, and then a long night working on linedefs and sidedefs, before I was displaying the complete map with lines and everything. I was mystified by vertexes that didn't seem to be used for anything, but I was very happy to see a Doom map on my screen.

It took many hours of plugging in numbers, entering Doom and looking around, and taking notes before I had found the raw object numbers for all the different types of THINGS. It didn't help that the numbers are not contiguous. That seemed like a diabolical plot to me at the time.

After a few days of neglecting "real work," I had a rudimentary thing editor working (Figure 1.1). I was completely unaware of external WAD files at this time, so the objects were being changed right in the IWAD itself.

Looking back now, it is amazing how far things have come. The editor is now a full-fledged application that does it all (see Figures 1.2 and 1.3), and literally thousands of new Doom WAD files have been created by player-authors.

I owe a lot of thanks to all the people who used the editor in the early days, and whose suggestions have made the present editor what it is, so different from its beginnings. The support of those early users was very heartening, and helped justify the long hours and

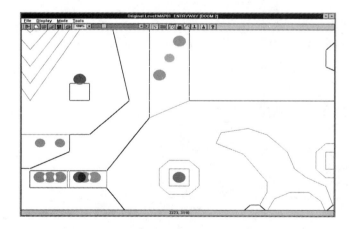

FIGURE 1.2

The Renegade Graphics Doom Editor Deluxe (included with this book).

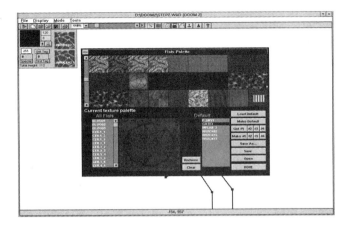

FIGURE 1.3

One of the many menus in the Doom Editor.

missed mundane work. Although the editor is only one small portion of my company's business, we all enjoy Doom so much that it gets lots of attention. I hope that you will enjoy using the editor as much as I enjoyed creating it.

Master WAD and
PWAD Structure

This chapter describes the technical details of the data structures that Doom uses to represent levels, sounds, graphics, and other vital information. It is not essential that you gain expert knowledge of the details— the editor handles the technical details and lets you concentrate on the creative aspects of level construction. But just as artists can be more competent when they fully understand their tools, you may find your level-building skills improved by reading through this chapter. The information will help you to understand what you are manipulating as you edit, and why there are certain limitations to what you can create. If you are interested in programming a utility that modifies Doom PWAD data in some way, you will find this information extremely useful.

 # The Gory Details

The Doom or Doom II you purchased came with a large file called DOOM.WAD or DOOM2.WAD. This file is known as the IWAD or, as it is also referred to in this book, the Master WAD.

When you use an editor or other utility that creates add-ons for Doom, you are creating a patch WAD or PWAD—the data it contains patches the IWAD. When Doom runs with PWAD files specified on the command line, it uses the data from those files as an overlay to the IWAD in memory. The result is that you can replace nearly any aspect of the IWAD data with a custom PWAD file that can be loaded as desired.

Unless otherwise stated, all information in this chapter applies to both PWAD and IWAD files.

Variable Types

Data stored in the WAD file is in the form of ASCII characters, integers (Ints), or long integers (Longs). ASCII characters are 1 byte each, Ints are 2 bytes each, and Longs are 4 bytes each. All strings in WAD files are 8 bytes long with no extraneous bytes.

WAD File Identification

The type of WAD file is identified by the first 4 bytes of the file. These will be the character string IWAD or PWAD.

The Directory

Immediately following the identification bytes at the start of the WAD are 2 Longs. These 2 Longs identify the number of entries in the directory and the first byte of the directory, respectively. The directory is normally located at the very end of the WAD, and it is good programming practice to keep it there.

Each entry in the directory is 16 bytes in length, made up of two Longs and a string. The first Long is a pointer to the start of the entry, the second Long is the length of the entry, and the string is the name of the entry. If the letter characters making up the name are fewer than 8, the remaining characters are filled with hex 00.

The directory in the IWAD file contains every single piece of data external to the executable that Doom makes use of for normal play (see Table 2.1).

Level Data

Each level is defined by an entry name for the level such as E1M1 or MAP01, followed by ten entries

TABLE 2.1	IWAD File Directory
Name	**Purpose**
PLAYPAL	Color palettes
COLORMAP	Remapping information for using the same palette for various levels of brightness
ENDOOM	Text message displayed when you exit Doom
DEMO1	An LMP used to show a demo game while no one is playing
E*n*M*n*	Start of level data entries (for Doom levels)
MAP*nn*	Start of level data entries (for Doom II levels)
TEXTURE1	List of wall textures and instructions to Doom on how to build them
TEXTURE2	List of wall textures and instructions to Doom on how to build them (Registered Doom only)
D_*name*	Music
DP_*name*	Sound effect data for PC speaker sound
DS_*name*	Sound effect data for digital sound
various	Block or full-screen graphics entries
S_START	Start of sprite graphics entries
various	Sprite graphics

TABLE 2.1	Continued
Name	**Purpose**
S_END	End of sprite graphics
P_START	Start of wall patches
P1_START	Start of patch group 1
P1_END	End of patch group 1
P2_START	Start of patch group 2 (Registered Doom only)
P2_END	End of patch group 2 (Registered Doom only)
P_END	End of wall patches
F_START	Start of flats (floor/ceiling textures)
F1_START	Start of flat group 1
F1_END	End of flat group 1
F2_START	Start of flat group 2
F2_END	End of flat group 2
F3_START	Start of flat group 3 (Doom II only)
F3_END	End of flat group 3 (Doom II only)
F_END	End of flats

(appearing in this order in the WAD file): THINGS, LINEDEFS, SIDEDEFS, VERTEXES, SEGS, SSECTORS, NODES, SECTORS, REJECT, and BLOCKMAP (see Tables 2.2 and 2.3).

The items in Table 2.3 are generated by the BSP program. This data is not edited directly by the person creating a level. The BSP is explained in Chapter 4.

TABLE 2.2	WAD Entries That Can Be Directly Modified by the DOOM Editor
Entry	**Definition**
THINGS	Monsters, player starts, equipment, etc.
VERTEXES	Points that define endpoints of lines
LINEDEFS	Lines
SIDEDEFS	Definitions of the sides of lines (walls)
SECTORS	Sector attributes

The first of the main entries, THINGS, is the only one that stands more or less on its own. All the other entries, including the generated ones, are interdependent (see Figure 2.1).

TABLE 2.3	WAD Entries That Are Generated from Other Data
Entry	**Definition**
SEGS	BSP data
SSECTORS	BSP data
NODES	BSP data
REJECT	Game optimization
BLOCKMAP	Game optimization

FIGURE 2.1

The interdependency

of the main entries.

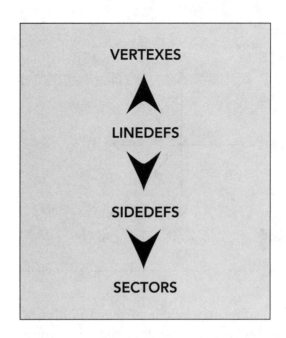

The coordinates of the level are defined only by the VERTEXES, and the heights are defined only by the SECTORS. The SECTORS data contains only the sector heights, floor and ceiling textures, and possibly a special attribute. The shape of the sector is defined by the sides that face it, and their locations are in turn defined by the line they are on; the line's position is defined by the vertexes it lies between.

This interdependency is further complicated when you deal with two-sided lines and special activations. If a line has only one side, that side must be the first side. The first side is defined as the side that would be on the right if you were facing in the direction the line travels from one vertex to another.

Some line specials can only be activated by travel through them in a particular direction. Examples of

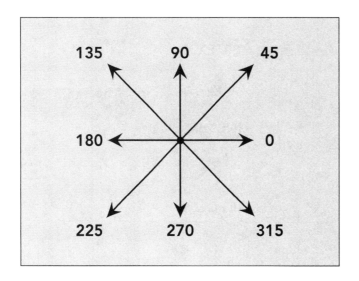

FIGURE 2.2

Thing facing values.

these are the specials that trigger teleporters and lifts. These lines are always two-sided so that there is some flexibility in which direction they go.

THINGS

Each thing is defined by 5 integers (10 bytes):

Int	X coordinate of thing
Int	Y coordinate of thing
Int	Angle the thing faces
Int	Type of thing
Int	Attributes of thing (bit field)

A level with 130 things on it will have 1300 bytes in its THINGS entry.

The facing values are shown in Figure 2.2. Values other than these will be rounded to the nearest value divisible by 45, so there is no point in using odd values.

Table 2.4 shows how the bit values of the attribute integer are used as flags to represent several attributes of a thing.

TABLE 2.4	Bit Values of the Attribute Integer
Bit	**Meaning**
0	Appears on skills 1 and 2
1	Appears on skill 3
2	Appears on skills 4 and 5
3	Deaf
4	Multiplayer only
5–15	Unused

VERTEXES

Vertexes define starting and ending points for Lines and Segs. Each vertex is an X,Y coordinate made of 2 integers (Ints).

LINEDEFS

A line is defined by 7 integers. Its location is defined by the vertexes drawn between. [The line also points to the side(s) it has facing any sector beside it.]

Int   From vertex (Vertexes are numbered from 0)

Int   To vertex

Int   Line attributes

Int   Line special

Int   Line tag

Int   Side 1 SideDef (required)

Int   Side 2 SideDef (two-sided sector only)

Line attributes are flags in a bit field. Any or all of the attributes may be set (see Table 2.5). The exact function of each attribute is explained in Chapter 5.

The Line Special, if any, defines what action that line performs on the sector or sectors whose tag number matches the tag number for this line. With the exception of Doors, any line that has a Special must also have a tag and sector that corresponds to that tag number. If the tag number is omitted, it is seen as a 0 and will affect every sector on the level. This is a bad thing because your level will not work properly. The Doom engine will be unable to locate a unique relationship between the activated line and a particular sector.

TABLE 2.5   Line Attributes

Bit	Meaning
0	Block Player
1	Block Monster
2	Two-sided
3	Float upper texture
4	Float wall texture
5	Secret for Automap
6	Block sound
7	No draw
8	Already on map
9–15	Unused

Lines that act as the front sides of Doors do not require a tag; they are automatically associated with the sector behind them.

The values of Side 1 and Side 2 point at SIDEDEFS. Side 1 must always point at one of the SIDEDEFS, while Side 2 may only point to a SIDEDEF if the line is two-sided.

If the line only has one side, it must never have its two-sided bit flag set. If it does, the wrong texture will be displayed for the wall, and the engine will be slowed trying to calculate the effects of a nonexistent sector.

Two lines may never point at the same SIDEDEF.

SIDEDEFS

The SIDEDEFS are structures that define a wall and point to the sector that the wall faces. Each entry in the SIDEDEFS is 2 integers, 3 strings, and another integer, totaling 30 bytes:

Int	X offset of wall texture
Int	Y offset of wall texture
String	Upper or "Ledge" texture name
String	Lower or "Step" texture name
String	Normal or "Wall" texture name
Int	Sector that this side faces

The X and Y offsets are used for shifting the wall texture within the space defined for it. Imagine a flat panel where the wall texture is going to be drawn. It is defined in width by the length of the line it runs along,

and in height by the difference in height of sectors in the case of Upper and Lower textures, or by the height of the sector it faces in the case of a Normal texture.

To shift the graphic to the right within the space, use a positive X offset. A negative offset moves the texture to the left.

To shift the graphic up on the wall, use a positive Y offset. Negative offsets will move the texture further down the wall.

The offsets are equal to the number of pixels the graphic should be shifted.

The texture names refer to items in the TEXTURE1 or TEXTURE2 directory entry.

The sector number points at the SECTORS entry of the sector that the sidedef on this side of the line faces.

SECTORS

The sector entry defines the floor and ceiling heights and textures, the brightness of the sector, and possibly a sector special and tag to associate the sector with a line. Each entry in the SECTORS is 2 integers, 2 strings, and 3 integers, totaling 26 bytes:

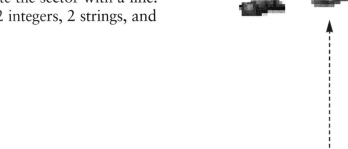

Int	Floor Height
Int	Ceiling Height
String	Floor Texture
String	Ceiling Texture
Int	Brightness
Int	Special
Int	Tag

Positive heights are up, negative are down. The floor height value must always be less than or equal to the ceiling height.

The names for the floor and ceiling textures are taken directly from the directory entries in the F_START to F_END section of the directory. Flat textures or flats are simple and do not go through any of the intermediate handling that the wall textures go through.

The brightness of a sector ranges between 0 and 255, 0 being complete darkness and 255 the brightest. There are only 32 graphic palettes for brightness, so values between 0 and 7 will all appear the same; thus, when you are adjusting the brightness value, it makes sense to do so in multiples of 8. Allowing 256 values is an example of forward thinking—when Doom is available on a more advanced graphics platform, the full range of brightness levels will be represented.

The Special value indicates if a sector has some special attribute, like flashing lights, or the fact that being in the sector causes damage to the player. The values that can be set here are defined in the editor.

If this sector is acted upon by a line special, the tag is used to associate it with that line. Any line that has a matching tag value will act upon this sector when it is triggered.

The tag value itself has no meaning; the number is completely arbitrary.

SEGS

Segs are defined during the BSP process. In the same way, lines and sides define a sector, and the SEGS

define SSECTORS, which are in turn a part of the NODES tree. Each entry in the SEGS is 6 integers, totaling 12 bytes:

Int	From vertex
Int	To vertex
Int	Angle
Int	LINEDEF this seg is on top of
Int	LINEDEF side
Int	Offset

Additional vertexes are inserted during the BSP phase for SEGS to make use of, along with the existing vertexes used by the lines.

The Angle is defined in BAMS (Binary Angle Measurement System). The hex values follow the pattern 0000 = East, 4000 = North, 8000 = West, C000 = South. The angle is computed from the inverse tangent of the distance between the x and y coordinates of the vertexes, adjusted so that PI/2 radians is equal to 16384.

The LINEDEF Side has a value of 0 or 1. If the Seg is for the first side of the line, the value is 0; if it is for the second side, the value is 1.

The Offset is the distance along the LINEDEF that this Seg starts. The Offset is from the From vertex toward the To vertex. If the Seg starts right at the From vertex, the Offset will be 0.

SSECTORS

Subsectors or SSECTORS are created during the BSP process and are analogous to sectors. Each entry in the

SSECTORS is 2 integers, totaling 4 bytes:

Int   Number of SEGS in the SSECTOR

IntFirst Seg Number in the SSECTOR

As part of the BSP process, the entire level must be carved up into subsectors that are convex polygons. If a sector is shaped such that from a vantage point within the sector a line that makes up the sector could obscure another line in that sector, the sector must be broken up into subsectors. The subsectors do not have to be a continuous shape, merely a group of lines within a single sector that do not obscure each other.

SSECTORS are pointed to by the NODES directory entry.

NODES

The NODES define the BSP tree and are created as part of the BSP process. Each entry in the NODES is 14 integers, totaling 28 bytes:

Int   X coordinate of partition line's start

Int   Y coordinate of partition line's start

Int   dX, change in X to end of partition line

Int   dY, change in Y to end of partition line

Int   Y upper bound for right bounding box

Int   Y lower bound

Int   X lower bound

Int   X upper bound

Int   Y upper bound for left bounding box

Int   Y lower bound

Int   X lower bound

Int	Upper bound
Int	a NODE or SSECTOR number for the right child
Int	a NODE or SSECTOR number for the left child

If the NODE or SSECTOR number is negative, then the branch below is an SSECTOR; otherwise it is a recursed node.

The nodes are branches in a BSP or binary space partition. The purpose of a BSP is to provide a fast method of determining what objects are in front of others from a given vantage point. In Doom, the BSP is used to determine what order to draw the walls in (from the farthest away to the closest).

The total BSP is made up by the NODES tree, the SSECTORS, and the SEGS.

The BSP as it relates to Doom is explained in Chapter 4.

REJECT

The REJECT entry is an array of bits, with the vertical and horizontal number of bits being equal to the number of SECTORS in the level. Thus, the byte length of the REJECT entry is (# of SECTORS)^2 /8.

Table 2.6 shows the bits of the sector that the player is in, indexed by the sector that a monster might try to observe the player from.

The purpose of the table is to reduce the amount of time spent calculating whether monsters see the player. If a 1 is present in the table, the engine can skip over

TABLE 2.6 Portion of an Example Reject Table

Sector Player is in

Sector Monster is in	0	1	2	3	4	5	6
0	0	0	0	0	1	0	0
1	1	0	0	0	0	0	0
2	0	0	0	1	0	1	0
3	0	0	1	0	0	0	0
4	1	0	0	0	0	0	1
5	0	0	1	0	0	0	0
6	0	0	0	0	1	0	0

1 = monster cannot view player

any monsters in that sector when the player is in the corresponding sectors.

The REJECT table is not required for a valid DOOM level. If it is not present, a table of all 0s will be assumed, and the engine will check normally for player detection.

BLOCKMAP

The BLOCKMAP is used to speed collision detection between things and walls. It is of variable size. All fields in the BLOCKMAP are integers:

Int   X minimum

Int   Y minimum

Int   X Blocks

Int   Y Blocks

followed by (X Blocks * Y Blocks) pointers:

Int   Pointer to Block 0 list

..

Int   Pointer to Block (X Blocks * Y Blocks) −1 list

followed by (X Blocks * Y Blocks) lists:

0   Start of Block n list

Int   LINEDEF in Block n − 1 End of Block n list

. . .

The BLOCKMAP divides the level up into 128×128 blocks. Each block list contains the numbers of all the LINEDEFS that cross any part of that block. When an object is checked for collision with walls, only the lines that are in the list for the block the thing is in need to be checked. This greatly speeds collision detection.

If a valid BLOCKMAP is not present in the level data, no lines will be found for collision detection. This will allow everything, including projectiles, to be able to go through walls. The block entries are listed in order from left to right, starting at the bottom left corner of the map and ending at the upper right corner.

The start and end of a block list are marked with a 0 and −1. Every block must be listed, even if it contains no lines. If a block is empty, its list will simply be 0 and −1.

The total size of the BLOCKMAP must be large enough to cover all the LINEDEFS that make up the level.

Graphics

All graphics in Doom make use of several graphics color palettes that vary in brightness to indicate an item has been picked up or have a red tinge to indicate the player is taking damage. These palettes are then mapped according to the brightness level the graphic is exposed to. The palettes are stored in the PLAYPAL resource, and only one palette is used at a time to display the entire screen. The COLORMAP resource contains mappings for various brightness levels within the same palette. Several different brightness levels (or all of them) can thus be shown on the screen at one time, while the entire color of the screen can be shifted rapidly to react to damage.

PLAYPAL

The PLAYPAL entry contains 14 palettes. Each palette is 256 colors, with 1 byte each for red green, and blue, or a total of 768 bytes. The total entry length is 10,752 bytes.

Table 2.7 shows when the palettes are used. When a player takes damage, there is a shift in palette to reflect the amount of damage, as indicated on this table. The normal palette is then returned to by way of the palette steps in between.

When a player picks up an item, the palette goes to 10. If another item is picked up while that palette is still being used, it will shift up again to 11, and so on.

COLORMAP

The graphics of Doom are designed using palette 0. These colors are then mapped during play onto other colors according to the brightness desired.

The COLORMAP directory entry contains 34 mappings. Each map is 256 bytes long. The byte position determines the color number that is remapped to the color number contained by the byte value. For the colormap that is used at the highest brightness levels, the colors are unchanged, so the byte values are equal to the byte numbers 0, 1, 2, 3, 4, 5, 6, . . , 254, 255.

TABLE 2.7	PLAYPAL Palettes
Palette	**Use**
0	Normal display
1	Unknown
2	16% damage
3	Berserk strength flash
4	35% damage
5	55% damage
6	81% damage
7	93% damage
8	100%+ damage
9	Unknown
10	Pick up brightness
11	Pick up brightness
12	Pick up brightness (brightest)
13	Radiation suit (green tinge)

At the darkest (lowest brightness), the COLORMAP is mapped entirely to blacks and grays.

The first 32 colormaps correspond to the 32 displayed levels of brightness. The COLORMAP following them is mapped entirely to shades of gray and is used when the player has Invulnerability. The last COLORMAP is all black.

PICTURES

All graphics other than those for floors and ceilings are stored in the same format. Each picture is defined by three sections of data, in a pattern similar to the BLOCKMAP; the sections of data are of various lengths.

Int	X size
Int	Y size
Int	X offset
Int	Y offset

The next data is a number of pointer offsets from the start of the picture data. There will be as many pointers as the value of X size.

Long	Pointer to pixel data for column 1
. . .	
Long	Pointer to pixel data for column (X size)

After the pointers are lists of pixel group data that correspond to the pointer list, and pixel columns of the graphic.

| Byte | Y start for this group of pixels |
| Byte | Number of pixels bytes that follow (n) |

followed by (n) + 2 bytes of pixels:

Byte   Color number (from palette) for this pixel

This may be followed by additional pixel group data:

255   End of pixel groups for this column

followed by pixel groups for the next column.

The X and Y size define the rectangular space in which the graphic is drawn. The X and Y offsets are used to achieve realistic effects and to keep sprite graphics tightly matched to the environment to prevent the "sliding" appearance of items in Wolf 3D.

Negative values for the X and Y offsets signal that the absolute values of the offsets mark the screen position at which the graphic should be drawn. This is used in the case of weapons that have a position relative to the screen and not the environment. The values are based on a screen size of 320×200 pixels and are scaled by the engine automatically for different screen sizes.

To float an object above the floor, a Y offset larger than the Y size is used. If an object rests on the ground, the Y offset should be set exactly equal to the Y size.

In the case of wall texture patches, the offsets are always set in the same manner: The X offset should be equal to (X size/2) – 1 and the Y offset should be equal to Y size – 5.

The pixel group information is scarier than it looks. In the case of a rectangular graphic with no transparent spaces, the number of pixel group blocks will be equal to the number of column pointers and the X size. The X size is the width of the graphic: For each pixel across the graphic there must be a column of pixel data and a pointer to the pixel data. It is only when a transparent area is needed within the rectangular space, such as in the case of

FIGURE 2.3 (Left)

A static,

unanimated object

FIGURE 2.4 (Right)

Two versions

of armor.

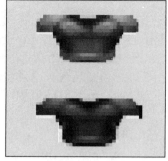

FIGURE 2.3 (Left)

A static,

unanimated object

FIGURE 2.4 (Right)

Two versions

of armor.

a sprite or a texture with a hole in it, that multiple pixel groups will be used in a single column of the picture.

In the case of a rectangular texture, the Y start will always be 0. A texture with a hole will also start at 0, but the first pixel group will stop at the top edge of the hole and the Y start of the following group will be the pixel below the gap. A graphic in the middle of the rectangle will have initial Y starts of 0 for many of its first pixel groups. Only those columns that start at the very top of the rectangle, such as the top of a Trooper's head, will have a Y start of 0.

Each column of pixel groups is terminated by a byte 255.

SPRITES

Sprite graphics are used to create the monsters, players, and other things that move in Doom. Sprite graphics follow a simple naming scheme. The first four characters of the directory entry are the sprite name. The next two characters indicate the sequence number and facing that the sprite represents for that thing.

In the case of a static un-animated object like a column, only one graphic is present, A0. Figure 2.3 shows an un-animated column (COLUA0).

In the case of a static animated object, there will be multiple letters indicating sequence, but they will all end in 0, indicating that the object has no particular facing. For example, Figure 2.4 shows an animated armor (ARM1A0 and ARM1B0).

Monster and Player graphics have not only an animation sequence, but also a number indicating the viewing side. Since objects can be viewed from 8 sides, you can draw 8 different images to represent an object. But there are some ways to *cheat*—you can reuse some images so that you don't have to draw so many. Graphic images that are designed to be viewed from a "diagonal" (positions 2, 4, 6, and 8) will usually be used twice, once in the position it is stored in, and once flipped horizontally. A graphic of a monster drawn to appear facing toward you and to the right will, when flipped, appear that the monster is facing toward you and to the left. In these cases there will be two sets of sequence and direction characters at the end of the name, as in SARGA2A8. In the case of the A8 viewing position, the graphic is horizontally flipped from the A2 position the graphic is originally drawn in.

Textures

In Doom the textures that are mapped onto vertical surfaces are completely different from those on flat surfaces. Flat surfaces never contain transparent portions and are always exactly 64 × 64 pixels. Textures used on vertical surfaces can be any size and are made up of graphic patches stored in a format that allows them to have transparent portions. The textures that appear on vertical surfaces are referred to as textures, while those on floors and ceilings are called *flats*.

TEXTURE1 AND TEXTURE2

These directory entries contain the names of the textures and instructions on how they are put together. Textures are built up out of patches. This method allows the same patch to be used in multiple textures, resulting in a savings in disk space and reducing the amount of data the engine has to search for. The items in the TEXTURE directory entry are of varying lengths, depending upon the number of patches a texture contains.

The TEXTURE entry starts with a Long value indicating the number of textures, followed by a list of pointers to the start (byte offset from the start of TEXTURE) of each texture description.

Each texture description consists of a block that indicates the size of the texture and the number of patches that make it up, followed by that many patch values and positions:

Int	0 (unused)
Int	0 (unused)
Int	X size
Int	Y size (max 256)
Int	0 (unused)
Int	0 (unused)
Int	Number of patch descriptions that follow (*n*)

The remaining data is (*n*) patch descriptions.

Int	X offset

Int	Y offset
Int	PNAMES entry number of this patch graphic
Int	1 (unused)
Int	0 (unused)

The X and Y offsets indicate the upper left corner of the patch relative to the upper left corner of the total texture. The Int number of the patch graphic relates directly to the PNAMES directory entry that assigns a number value to each of the patch graphic names in the WAD file.

PNAMES

PNAMES starts with an integer that indicates the number of strings that follow. The rest of PNAMES is a list of all patch names. The order in the list indicates the number that is used in the TEXTURE data to refer to each patch.

The entries are not case sensitive.

Flats

The names of flat textures used in the SECTORS definitions are exactly the names used for the graphics in the F_START to F_END block of the directory.

The flats are simple graphics with no special tricks like transparent spaces. Flats are always 64 × 64 pixels and each flat entry is 4096 bytes long, each byte corresponding to a palette entry.

The first byte is the upper left corner of the graphic; the data then runs left to right, with rows reading top to bottom.

The F_SKY1 graphic is not used anywhere besides the editor. The F_SKY1 texture signals to the engine to draw the sky using the appropriate bitmap in a special method that gives the sky its appearance of separation.

Music and Sound

The entries related to music and sound are the simplest to deal with because they are standard format files imbedded into the WAD.

MUSIC

Entries that follow the pattern D_xxxxx are music. They are simply a file in the MUS format imbedded directly into the WAD.

SOUND

Entries following the patterns DP_xxxxx and DS_xxxxx are sound effects. The DP sound effects are used when PC speaker sound is selected. The DS sound effects are used when a sound card is selected.

The DS entries are in RAW format. The first 4 bytes are integer values and are always the same except for the sample length. The four Ints are, in order, 3, the sample rate (usually 11025), the length, and 0.

Demos

The entries DEMO1 through DEMO3 are the demonstration games played when Doom is left unattended. These are simply LMP files imbedded directly into the WAD. LMP files are recorded with the developer parameter −RECORD.

Doom will only look for demos with the names
DEMO1 through DEMO3.

What's in the WAD, What's Not

While a great deal of what makes up Doom is stored in
the WAD files, there are many important things that
are not. The information governing the behavior of all
objects within Doom is defined within the executable.
This includes the amount of damage an item can with-
stand, its speed, and other attributes such as whether it
can explode or take damage.

Many of these attributes can be modified by "hacking"
the Doom executable with a program such as DE-
HACKED. Details of this program are in Chapter 7.

 The Difference Between Doom and Doom II IWADs

The IWAD structures for Doom and Doom II are nearly identical. There are only two differences. The Doom
II IWAD contains many more entries due to the
increased number of sprites and sounds. The other difference is the designation of the level by a MAPxx
entry instead of ExMx.

Beginning to Build
Your Own Levels

The Original Levels

According to John Carmack of id Software, over a year of person-hours went into the editing of the 27 levels for the original Doom. That works out to a bit over 70 hours of work *for each level.* Of course, the people at id were starting from scratch, and editing tools were not as advanced as they are today. Still, while it is true that you can be walking around your own level ten minutes after you first run the editor, it will take some time for you to create a masterpiece.

The original Doom levels are "classic" levels; you do not need to find any secret areas to complete a level, there are no dead ends, and (despite how it may seem at times) there are no impossible situations. Chapters 3 and 5 focus on the techniques that make up 95 percent of editing, and on "classic" level creation. These techniques must be mastered before any advanced and non-classic levels can be created.

If you haven't already installed the editor, you should

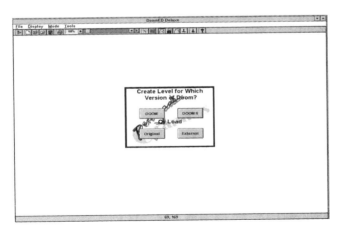

FIGURE 3.1

The opening screen of the Doom Editor.

do so before continuing. See Appendix A for detailed instructions.

 # Orientation

Let's begin with something familiar—the first level of Doom II. (Note that while MAP01 of Doom II is used as the example, the principles are applicable to any level.) After you enter the editor, select Original (see Figure 3.1).

You will be presented with a dialog that lets you choose which original Doom level you want to load. If you have Doom II, the editor will appear exactly as shown in Figure 3.2; otherwise, the editor will, by default, load E1M1 of Doom. In either case, hit OK.

The level will be loaded, and will be displayed centered and at the default level of magnification (see Figure 3.3; the display will appear somewhat different if you are using Windows at a screen resolution other than the 1024 × 768 resolution used for this book).

FIGURE 3.2

Loading a

Doom II level.

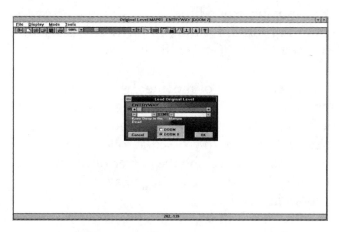

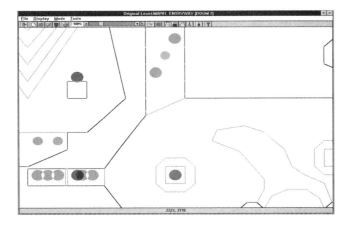

FIGURE 3.3

A Doom level fully loaded into the editor.

Take a moment to orient yourself. The colored circles represent monsters and items (hereafter referred to as "things"). Move your pointer around the screen. Notice that the help bar at the bottom of the screen is constantly updated with various kinds of status information. When you are over the map, it displays coordinates or information about the nearest thing. When you are over a control, it displays information about what that control does.

Move around the map a bit. Notice that there are no scroll bars for the map. This has been done to save screen space—a valuable commodity at any screen resolution. Try moving around the map using the arrow keys on your keyboard. Pressing the arrows will move the screen one quarter of its width at a time.

Now try another method of moving: by centering on the cursor. This is done by pressing C and then clicking on the new center of the display. As soon as you press C the cursor will change to crossed arrows. The next location you click will become the center of the display. If you hold the Shift key when you press C, the map will also zoom in a little.

The map has many different possible levels of zoom. The simplest way to change the current zoom for the display is with the + and − keys. Normally the zoom will change by a factor of 10. To zoom more quickly, hold down the Shift key for a zoom factor of 20, the Ctrl key for a zoom factor of 30, and the Alt key for a zoom factor of 40.

There is also a miniature map control (see Figure 3.4). This control shows a small version of the map and allows you to relocate the display simply by clicking on it.

The map control is summoned by pressing Ctrl+X. The first time you use it in each session it will appear in the center of the screen. You may move it off to one side if you prefer; if you have a large display, you may choose to resize the main window so that you can see the map control all the time.

The map control is simple to use. You can see the entire map at one time and click on the area you wish to move to. The rectangle on the display always reflects the currently viewed area on the main display (see Figure 3.5).

FIGURE 3.4

The miniature map control.

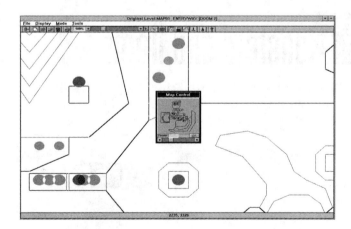

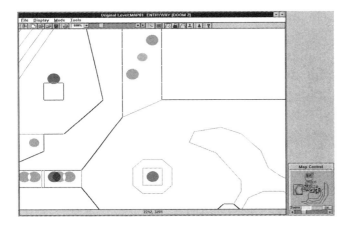

FIGURE 3.5

Using the map control.

Practice using these methods to navigate around the map.

The editor has three basic modes: Object editing, Special/Texture editing, and Structure editing. The easiest way to change between these modes is with the buttons on the toolbar (see Figure 3.6). The leftmost of these three icons selects Object editing, the middle icon selects Special/Texture editing, and the rightmost icon selects Structure editing. Use them now and switch between the modes to see how the map display changes in appearance.

 # Monsters and Items

When you are in Object editing mode you are concerned only with the objects themselves. The structure

FIGURE 3.6

Toolbar buttons for changing modes.

of the map is secondary and only needs to be indicated, not manipulated. The objects are displayed as circles of various sizes and colors.

The sizes indicate the actual sizes of the objects within the game. Size must be considered together with placement to avoid problems in the game. Monsters placed too close to each other or to a wall will be stuck and unable to attack. If two monsters are placed too close to each other, when one monster is killed the survivor will become unstuck. If a monster is too close to a wall, however, it will never be able to move or attack. Table 3.1 shows the sizes of the player and monsters in pixels.

Seeing the size of things is also helpful when you are fitting them into small places. Monsters cannot traverse

TABLE 3.1		Vital Thing Sizes in Pixels
Radius	**Height**	**Type of Thing**
16	56	Player
20	56	Trooper
20	56	Sergeant
20	56	Imp
30	56	Demon/Specter
24	64	Hell Baron
31	56	Cacodemon
16	56	Lost Soul
10	42	Green Barrel
40	10	Cyberdemon
128	100	Spiderdemon

hallways that are not wider than they are. Things like lamps and barrels will look bad if placed so close to a wall that the graphics are clipped.

Manipulating Objects

To move a thing on the display, simply grab it with your pointer and drag it to the new location. If objects overlap, a combination of the display colors will be shown in the overlapping area so that you can be precise about placement.

Monsters should not be placed too close to each other, but other items do not suffer the same limitations. A monster and an item can be placed right on top of each other with no adverse effects. Items such as lamps and potions can be packed as tightly as you like, the only problem being their appearance in the game. In the detail from MAP06, "The Crusher," shown in Figure 3.7, you can see some typical overlapping of objects.

Center the display on the first room of MAP01 (see Figure 3.8). Move the pointer around and look at the

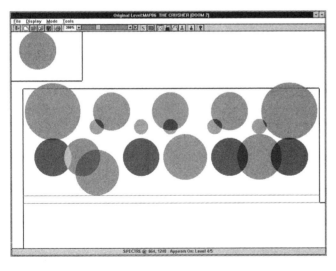

FIGURE 3.7

You can place monsters and items as close as you want.

FIGURE 3.8

Centering on the

first room in

MAP01.

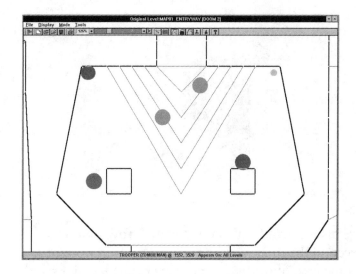

changing information displayed in the help bar. The precise coordinates of each object are given, as well as a plain English description of the item and when the item will appear in the game.

There are six items in the room; two of them are monsters. Of the other four items, only one will appear in a DeathMatch showdown. The BFG9000 next to the left-hand column is stock, to make network play a little more interesting.

Try moving things by clicking and dragging. Be careful not to leave something poking into a wall or, in the case of monsters, into another object.

Now let's change an object. To inspect or modify an existing item, click on it with the second mouse button. An inspection window will appear over the item (Figure 3.9).

The description of the thing is given, as well as the graphic used to represent the thing in the game. Several attrib-

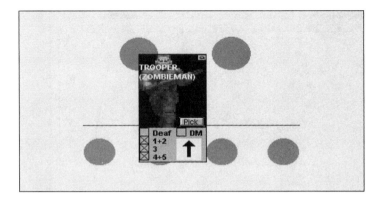

FIGURE 3.9

The inspection window.

utes are also shown for this thing. The arrow indicates the direction the thing will be facing. This is important only in the case of monsters and player start locations; other types of things are not affected by their facing.

To change the facing of this monster, click on the side of the arrow you want him to face. There are eight directions used in Doom.

The other attributes are shown as checkboxes. The numbered checkboxes indicate which difficulty levels the item will appear on. The difficulty levels "I'm Too Young to Die" and "Hey, Not Too Rough" are represented by 1–2, "Hurt Me Plenty" is 3, and "Ultraviolence" and "Nightmare" are difficulty levels 4–5.

Any or all of these difficulty settings may be selected. There are ways to make strategic use of these settings when you are designing a level. Typically, you will have first aid packs and other forms of help such as ammunition or better weapons available only at the lower difficulty settings, and more difficult monsters only on the higher settings. You might place a Trooper that appears on difficulties 1–2 and 4–5 right next to a Sergeant that appears on 3 and 4–5. This strategy of monster placement with difficulty level is evident throughout Doom; inspect the monsters on E1M1 for an example. This makes the challenge go up steadily.

The remaining two attributes are Deaf and DM. The Deaf attribute causes a monster to completely ignore sound. The only way a monster with this attribute set will "wake up" is if you shoot it or it sees your shots impact on a wall in its view. This is very useful for setting up a monster that can surprise a player by charging from around a corner when it sees gunfire. By making monsters deaf, you can prevent them from wandering off when they hear a noise in another part of the level.

The DM setting indicates that the item will appear in network games only. This attribute takes effect *regardless of what other switches are set for the item*. This means that any item with the DM switch set will *not* appear when you are testing or playing your level in a single-player game. This setting is used to stock a level with extra goodies for DeathMatch, like big guns and more ammo.

To change the object type of the currently inspected thing, click on the Pick button. A list of categories of

FIGURE 3.10

The inspection window with category of things.

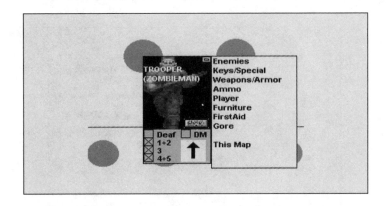

things will be displayed (see Figure 3.10). Choosing from this list is much easier than wading through a list of 120 or so types.

After you select a category, a list of things in that category will be displayed (Figure 3.11). As you scroll through the list, the graphic used to represent each thing is displayed along with its description. When you find the type of thing you want to change to, double-click on it. The thing type is changed.

Inserting and Deleting Objects

Object editing has two sub-modes: Move/Inspect and Insert/Delete. Whenever you switch to Object editing by using the icon on the toolbar, you will be in Move/Inspect mode. Switch to Insert/Delete mode by pressing I on your keyboard. You can also go directly to inserting and deleting objects by pressing this key from Structure mode or any other mode.

When you are in Insert/Delete mode, you can switch back to Move/Inspect by pressing T or clicking on the status bar at the bottom left of the display.

When you start Insert/Delete mode, the box used to

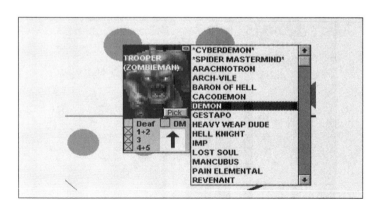

FIGURE 3.11

Double-click on a thing name to select it.

inspect things will appear in the upper left corner of the screen. Select the type of thing and the attributes you want. Next, click anywhere on the map to insert the thing. You may insert as many things as you like, moving around the map and clicking to insert them. Make sure you have selected the correct attributes.

To delete an item, click on it with the second (right) mouse button. You may move around the map and remove as many things as you like simply by right-clicking on them.

 # Basic Lighting

Effective lighting can make the difference between an OK level and a great level. Remember the first time you played Doom and you came to a dark hallway, with nearly black rooms and erratically flickering lights that brought to mind the movie *Aliens* (see Figure 3.12)?

If you botch the lighting, an otherwise nicely textured and furnished level can be tiresome or annoying.

FIGURE 3.12

Dark hallways with flickering lights add excitement.

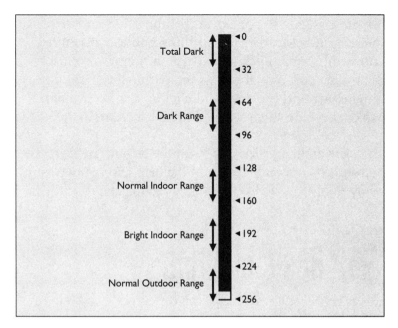

FIGURE 3.13

The range of

lighting levels

Lighting should be planned as the level is created. Consider where the light is coming from and work with it accordingly.

A common mistake is to make your levels *too* dark. Darkness should be used for effect when appropriate. Entire levels that are all dark and spooky wear thin after a while—the darkness loses its impact. A large number of extremely dark rooms is downright annoying. In the original E1M3, "Toxin Refinery," you got a big nasty surprise when you picked up the blue key and the lights went out. In E1M5, "Phobos Lab," you should recall a room that plunges you into blackness, leaving you almost helpless against a horde of pink demons. These were effective because the levels were not dark before then.

Brightly lit indoor areas can look sterile. A good typical indoor brightness is 144, with 128–160 being the range of normal indoor lighting (see Figure 3.13). Given the choice, a player will usually explore well-lit and open areas first. Keep that in mind when planning level flow.

Portions of a level that are outdoors or are lit by windows to the outdoors should have some considerable impact on the lighting. Outdoor areas should have a brightness between 224 and 255.

Room lighting can appear to come from outdoors, from the ceiling, or from wall panel lights and torches. Where the light is coming from affects how it should be handled and shaped. The light in Figure 3.14 is supposed to be coming from the panel of lights across the upper wall of the room. This explains the sharp change in brightness between the sectors.

A very nice effect both for lighting and for general appearance is a hole in the ceiling (see Figure 3.15). The simplest skylight of this sort is a sector with no wall textures, a higher ceiling and brightness than the sector around it, and appropriate textures on the upper wall.

Another very effective simple lighting technique is to use multiple sectors in the same map area for different levels of brightness. The source of the light should be obvious to the player for this to be effective. A good

FIGURE 3.14

Overhead panel lighting.

FIGURE 3.15

*A skylight
in E2M1.*

example of this is the first large room on MAP06 (see Figure 3.16) which uses this technique to create a very effective combination of light and shadow. A lamp or torch is set into an alcove in a wall or pillar, and sectors are created that follow the edge of the light path.

Notice that the sectors that are casting the light aren't perfectly straight (see Figure 3.17). By changing the angle of the lighter sector at the corner of the columns, a second shadow seems to be cast. This could be enhanced further by using multiple sectors with varying brightness levels to create the effect of overlapping shadows or areas of brightness.

FIGURE 3.16

*Multiple sectors
are used for a light
casting effect.*

FIGURE 3.17

Detail of MAP06

lighting effect.

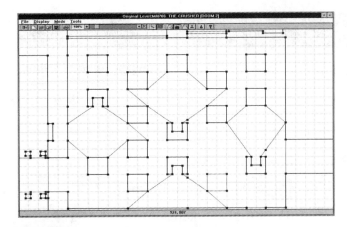

FIGURE 3.17

Detail of MAP06

lighting effect.

 # Sector Specials

The sector special is completely independent of any line special or tag relationship. The special attribute affects the entire sector, and only one such value may be assigned to a sector (see Table 3.2).

Sector specials are mainly used for lighting effects and to cause damage to the player. Damage-causing specials are generally used in nonwater pools so that the player can avoid them, but can be used anywhere you see fit.

 # The Process of Level Design

Your method of creating levels will depend on your personality. You may like to plan out everything ahead of time with pencil and paper, or you might just jump right into the editor and start dropping in sectors.

You will usually be starting from some particular inspiration—perhaps something you saw in a movie, or an interesting nightmare.

TABLE 3.2 Sector Special Values
(bold entries available in Doom II only)

Behavior	Sector Special Value
Nothing	0
−5% Health per second (Nukage)	7
−10% Health per second (Hell Slime)	5
−20% Health per second (Super Hell Slime)	16
Light blinks randomly (Light Flickering)	1
Light pulses each 1/2 second (Light Fast Strobe)	2
Light pulses each second (Light Slow Strobe)	3
−20% Health and Light pulses 1/2 second (Damage SuperStrobe)	4
Light varies between FULL brightness and adjacent (Light Glowing)	8
SECRET Counter credit (affects end level stats only)	9
−20% Health—used in ExM8 to end the episode (Exit Super Damage)	11
Pulsates between assigned brightness and 0 (Light Synch Strobe Slow)	12
Light blinks each 1/4 second (Light Synch Strobe Fast)	13
Ceiling Crush and Raise	6
Door closes in 30 seconds	10
Door raises in 5 minutes	14
Light Fire flickering	17

The editor lets you set the attributes of sectors you are about to draw, which makes things easy when you want to just sit down and create. You can plunk down a big room or two, throw in a few hallways and doors, and be walking around in your world in just a few minutes. Boring, but at least a place to start.

However, because of the intricacies of connecting and nesting sectors, a certain amount of planning is important and will minimize the amount of backtracking you might have to do. You should build one level at a time, room by room. Although general monster stocking can be left until the very end, at an earlier stage you might need to place monsters that are an integral part of a trap. Light source objects like lamps and torches are often important to the structure and should also be placed early.

Here are some guidelines for the design process:

1. Plan the level or start drawing chaotically, to suit your style.

2. As you add each room, consider:
  • Its relationship to the rooms that adjoin it
  • Its light level and the source of the lighting

3. Play the level. Check for:
  • Textures that look awful because of poor choice or alignment
  • Objects that are clipped because of bad placement or sector size
  • Monsters that are stuck or don't respond appropriately
  • Graphics errors (HOM, slowdowns)
  • Bad lighting

- Problems with line specials, teleporters that go the wrong way, lifts that don't work

4. Check the doors: make sure they are the right width to look good, that they use the right color key, and that they stay open or closed as you intended.

5. Fix the problems you find. Add more rooms and repeat.

6. Check the monster and item stocking at various difficulty levels.

7. Don't forget the exit!

8. Put a final polish on the level with the Reject utility. This will speed up large levels.

9. Play the level carefully without cheating, making sure that every area of the level can be reached properly. It's important to play without cheating so you can be sure that keys are accessible. Also consider the amount of support equipment (ammo and first aid): Is it adequate at the various difficulty settings?

10. Always have a few friends play through a level before uploading it to a BBS. You know the level perfectly, so of course you won't have any problem finding hidden doors and exits. But mere mortals may have considerable trouble. There may be problems with the level that you simply don't realize exist; or perhaps a last-minute change is causing a problem with something that was working just fine the last time you played the level.

11. Send masterpieces to Renegade Graphics BBS!

How to Build Your First Level

This level will be very basic, certainly nothing you would brag about on a BBS. It will contain the most essential elements of a level and let you actually walk around in something you created quickly.

We'll begin working at the default zoom level, Snap-to size (8), and Grid size (32). The screen shots in the figures are at 1024×768 with 64k colors; the display will look different at other display resolutions.

The zoom level is calculated relative to actual pixels on your screen. When the map is at 100% zoom, each pixel on your screen corresponds exactly to one pixel (measurement unit) in the game. Because of this, if you are using a 640×480 screen at the same zoom level, you will see approximately one-fourth as much of the map as I do at 1024×768. The same amount of detail is visible, though, and that is what is important. Calculating the zoom in this fashion keeps the feel of the editor the same at any screen resolution.

I usually keep the grid on when I am designing the structure and turn it off at other times. I find a visible grid size of 32 convenient because it fits the size of typical structures well; a small door is 64 wide and a large door is 128 wide. When I am aligning things to the flat textures, I set the grid to 64. At that size, one grid square is exactly aligned with the flats.

Don't worry if you don't create the shapes and sizes of the structures precisely as they are shown in the book. The process itself is the most important thing. Just be sure you connect the sectors properly.

Start the editor and choose the version of Doom you are going to create a level for. If you have only one version of Doom, the editor will default to that one. You should be in Structure mode. If you aren't, change to it by pressing V.

We'll begin with the place where the player will start. When the editor has just been started, the center of the display is at coordinate 0,0 and the zoom is 100%. Turn on the visible grid by clicking on the toolbar or pressing G. Locate the coordinate 0,0 by moving your mouse around and watching the coordinates on the help bar at the bottom of the display.

Pick the Sector tool—the icon is simply a square on an icon button. If you have difficulty locating it, keep your eye on the help bar at the bottom of the screen— it will say "Insert New Sector or Void" when you move over the right icon.

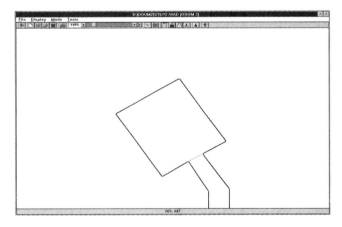

FIGURE 3.18

Dragging out a new sector.

FIGURE 3.19

The newly inserted sector extends from –64,–64 to 64,64.

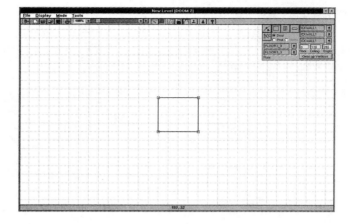

Drag out a new sector 128 wide and 128 high, centered on 0,0. To do this, move the pointer above and to the left of 0,0 until you are at –64,64. Hold down the mouse button and drag the dashed square down and to the right until the display says the width and height are both 128 (see Figure 3.18).

When you release the mouse button, a new sector is inserted. Your display should now look something like Figure 3.19.

Most of the original Doom levels start you out in a place where it looks as though you had just come in through a door or a window. The typical "start door" uses the 64 wide texture DOOR3. The door should be inset into the wall with another sector so that its height is controlled by that smaller sector and is independent of the height of the room sector it faces (see Figure 3.20). The start door isn't a real door at all, just a picture of one. There is nothing on the other side. Draw a sector 64 wide and 16 deep.

The door texture will be painted on the bottom line of the new sector. The height of the sector can be set to be exactly the height of the door texture, to make it look good.

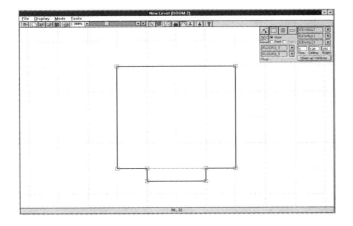

FIGURE 3.20

***A 64 × 16
entryway is
inserted.***

Next, create a larger room to the east (right). Make it about six times larger than the first room (see Figure 3.21). Let's put a hallway and a door between these two rooms. We can let the editor do the hard part. The icon to the right of the Sector tool is the AutoStruct tool. This can be used to automate creation of more complex structures like doors and pools.

Click on the AutoStruct icon, and then click again with the second (right) mouse button. This will display the AutoStruct Preferences (Figure 3.22). This is where you set up the type of door or pool to insert, and its orientation.

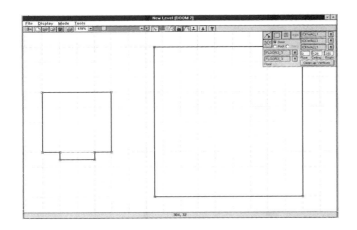

FIGURE 3.21

***A larger room
is created to
the east.***

FIGURE 3.22

FIGURE 3.22

The AutoStruct tool

Preferences.

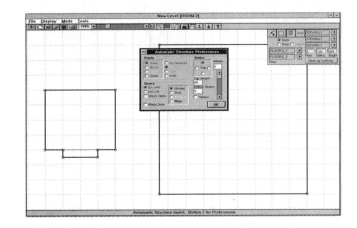

We need a door that opens between east and west
is normal (no key). The door will be placed in the center of whatever size rectangle you draw out. If you
wanted the door in the middle of the hall between the
two rooms, you would drag it out between them, but
in this case, let's place the door to be closer to the large
room (see Figure 3.23).

Presto! An instant door. Notice that in this case we
made it 64 wide from top to bottom. The AutoStruct
tool will allow you to draw a door any width you like,
but if you intend to use a DOOR texture, you should

FIGURE 3.23

Automated door

insertion.

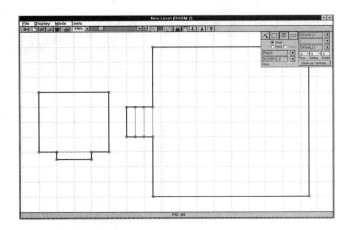

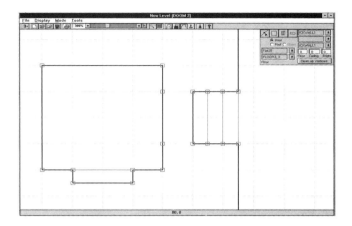

FIGURE 3.24

Break the wall in two places.

make it either 64 or 128 wide, since those are the widths the DOOR textures come in. Keep an eye on the height and width being displayed on the help bar as you draw the door; this will make it easy to make the door the precise width you want.

Now we need to connect to the smaller room. We have two options: We can either insert an additional sector between the stub end of the new door and the small room, or change the shapes to match up.

Since we don't have any plans for something that would require an additional sector in between, and

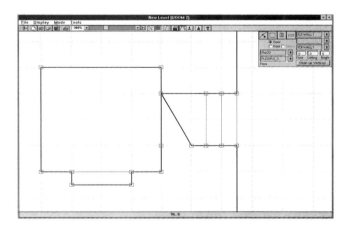

FIGURE 3.25

The first two vertexes are joined.

keeping in mind that the simpler we keep the level structures, the faster Doom will play, let's choose the second option. First, break the line that is the east wall of the small room. This is done with the vertex tool by right-clicking the line in two spots (see Figure 3.24). This break is where the door alcove sector will join.

The breaks don't have to be precise, because once they are made you can move them around easily with the mouse. Line up the vertexes that you just added with the alcove's vertexes. Then drag the vertexes from the alcove sector over to meet the vertexes you just created. If they are dropped close to one another, they will join (Figure 3.25).

When you move the second vertex so that a second pair of vertexes join, the two lines will join (Figure 3.26). Notice that the line is now displayed thin to indicate that it is interior—it lays between two sectors. The connection is now continuous between the hallway and the smaller sector.

Let's take a quick look at what has been done so far. A Player One object has to be inserted before you can load the level into Doom. Switch to Insert/Delete Thing

FIGURE 3.26

The second two vertexes, and the sectors, are joined.

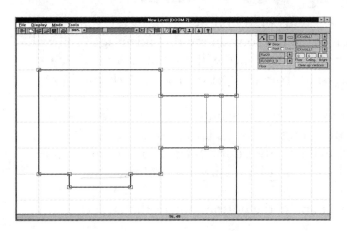

71

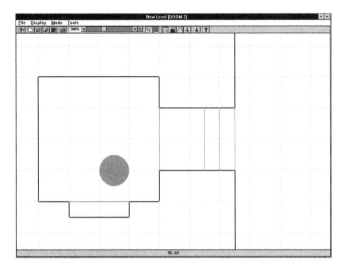

FIGURE 3.27

A Player One start is inserted into the level.

mode by pressing I. Pick a Player One start and set it to appear at all difficulty levels. Then insert it into the smaller room as shown in Figure 3.27.

Choose the disk icon from the toolbar or File/Save from the menu. A dialog box gives you a choice of what level to save this WAD as. See Chapter 4 for details on saving and loading new levels and for help if you get an error message or things onscreen look strange.

Adding Wall Textures

The new level is pretty boring so far. Everything is very bright and bland. You can see the indent into the wall where the false entrance will go, but there is little to distinguish it from the rest of the room (Figure 3.28).

Let's make a few minor improvements before we add any more structure to the level. Load the WAD you just created into the editor. Switch to Special/Texture mode by pressing P or using the toolbar.

Click just above the bottom line of the false entrance.

FIGURE 3.28

FIGURE 3.28

The player's view of

our Doom level.

The sector will be highlighted in green, the line will be highlighted in red, and boxes will appear displaying information about the sector, line, and side you have selected (see Figure 3.29). If you click just below the same line, you will notice that only the line is highlighted, and only the box with information about the line appears. The controls in this mode are context-dependent and will only appear when appropriate to what you have selected.

We'll paint this wall with the DOOR3 texture. The walls beside it could use some sprucing up as well.

FIGURE 3.29

Special/Texture

mode.

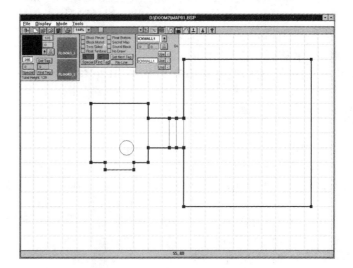

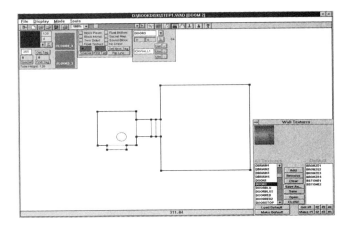

FIGURE 3.30

The Wall

Textures dialog.

Remember that they are 16 wide. (You can see the width of a line when you click on it—a number is displayed in the Side information box.)

Before we can paint the walls, we need to add those textures to our palette, assuming they aren't already in it. There are two palette choosers, and two icons used for viewing the choosers. The icons display small wall and floor grids in red or green. The icon on the Side information box has a red wall and green floor, signifying that it is for walls. The icon on the Sector information box has the reverse—a green wall and red floor.

Click on the icon for the wall texture. The Wall Textures dialog will appear and indicate what version of Doom you are currently editing by displaying the Doom or Doom II logo (Figure 3.30).

We need to add the DOOR3 texture. Click on the list that displays All Textures and scroll down to the doors. Locate DOOR3 and click on it. The texture is shown along with the size, 64 × 72. This is just right, since to look good, the door should be on a wall that is 72 high. Click on the Add button and the texture name is added to the list on the right.

FIGURE 3.31

The new textures have been added to the list.

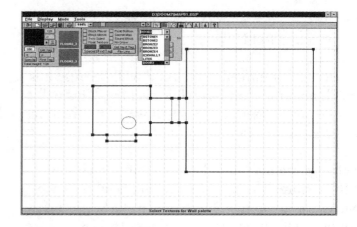

We also need a texture for beside the door. A good one would be LITE5, because it is 16 wide. Find it and add it to the palette.

Pick CLOSE and return to the editor. Make sure you have the wall that will have the door on it selected, then locate the DOOR3 texture in the wall texture drop-down list (Figure 3.31).

Click on the middle Use button to change the texture; in this example, you are changing from the previous texture (ICKWALL1) to DOOR3 (Figure 3.32).

FIGURE 3.32

The wall texture has been changed to DOOR3.

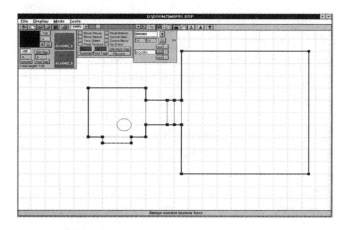

Follow the same procedure to change the sides of the false door sector to LITE5.

If you ever find it difficult to select a wall because it is too small, hold the Shift key while clicking. This will make it possible to select very small walls, but requires you to be more accurate.

Now change the height of that sector to match the DOOR3 texture. The floor and ceiling heights of the current sector are in the blue boxes in the Sector information box. The ceiling is currently set to 128; change it to 72.

The sector brightness levels are all at 255 right now, which makes things look sterile and washed out. Change them to more reasonable levels. You can quickly change the brightness level of the currently selected sector with the left bracket ([ ) and right bracket ( ]) keys. The left bracket will decrease brightness and the right bracket will increase it. The brightness normally changes by 8. Holding down the Shift key while you press the bracket keys will cause the brightness to change by 1, while holding the Alt key causes the brightness to be changed by 32.

Set the brightness of the small room to 167, the false door to 183, and everything else to 159. It is rather tedious to set the sector brightness for even these few sectors by hand. You should learn from this that it is wise to set the brightness as you create new sectors, not afterwards. Later you will learn how to use the Quick Paint tool to change the brightness or other attributes of many sectors quickly.

With these few cosmetic changes made, it's time to save the level and take another look (see Figure 3.33).

FIGURE 3.33

The room looks much better now.

Voids

So far you have created a few rooms, added an alcove to a room, and inserted a door. Sectors can contain areas that are not part of any sector—"voids." These are used to create columns and other solid wall areas. It is important to learn to make creative use of voids. Voids are drawn in the editor by using the second (right) mouse button with the Sector tool. Notice that the lines drawn are thick, to signify that they only have one side (see Figure 3.34). Only walls with nothing behind them are truly solid for the purposes of monster line-of-sight and firing.

FIGURE 3.34

Two voids are inserted as columns.

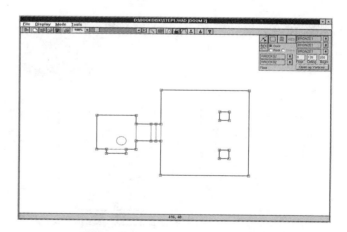

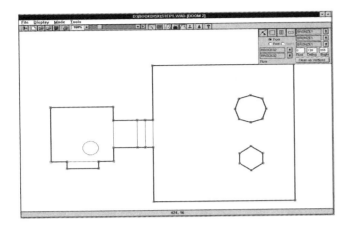

FIGURE 3.35

The columns are deformed into a hexagon and an octagon.

Make sure the Snap-to grid is set to 8 points by right-clicking on the Snap icon with the mouse. Now deform the shape of the columns by making them into hexagons or octagons (see Figure 3.35). Choose the Vertex tool and break some of the lines, then move the vertexes to get the shape you want.

Switch the AutoStruct radio button to Pool. Choose the AutoStruct tool, then right-click for preferences and choose a Lava pool that does 10% damage per second. Draw it to the left of the columns (Figure 3.36).

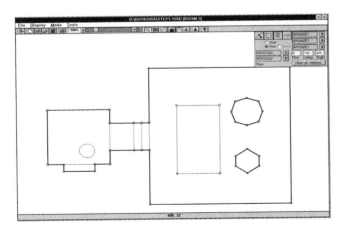

FIGURE 3.36

A new pool is inserted.

FIGURE 3.37

The new pool is reshaped.

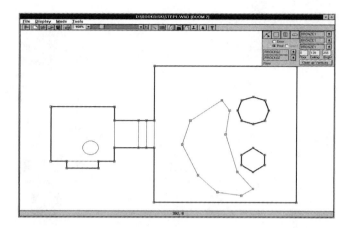

Choose the Vertex tool, and break up the sides of the pool to make the shape more interesting (Figure 3.37). Be careful not to let any lines cross each other.

Adding Another Room

Figures 3.38 through 3.44 demonstrate how you can build another large room to the north of the first room. First make the room itself (Figure 3.38). Then put a hallway between the two rooms (Figure 3.39). If you draw the hallway carefully, it will attach to the rooms automatically. Suppose that you want the new

FIGURE 3.38

Draw in another large room.

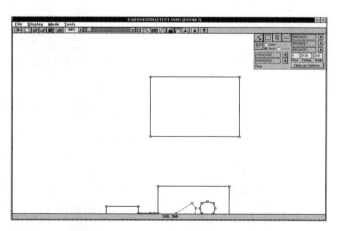

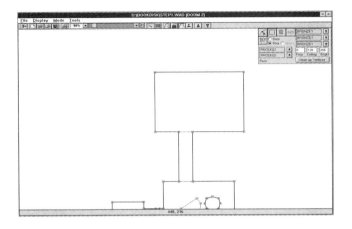

FIGURE 3.39

Carefully draw the hallway between the two rooms.

room to be rectangular, but at an angle to the other rooms. Once the rough structure is drawn in, the vertexes are moved into the approximate position of the new room. Then the grid and close zoom are used to position everything precisely (Figures 3.40–3.44).

If you want to be certain that the walls of this skewed room are at right angles to each other, turn on the grid and look closely at the rise and run of the lines. If lines in one direction travel two squares horizontally (run) for each square they travel vertically (rise), the lines at right angles to them should run one square for each two squares of rise.

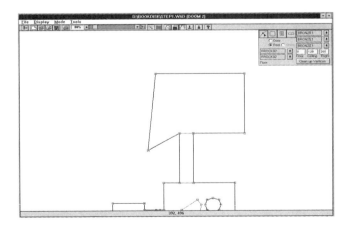

FIGURE 3.40

Deform the wall to approximately the angle you want.

FIGURE 3.41

Start moving the opening.

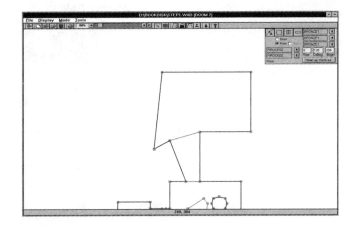

FIGURE 3.42

Moving the opening.

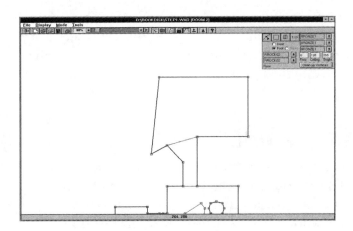

FIGURE 3.43

Moving the opening further.

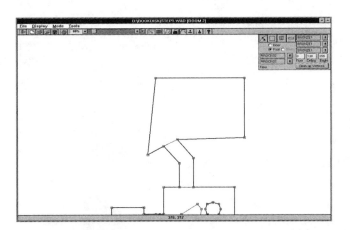

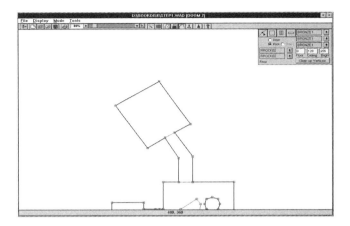

Set the visible gridlines to 64 (Figure 3.45). This will let you see the alignment of the flats. If you draw a sector exactly on this grid, the floor and ceiling textures will be perfectly aligned. This is useful for lights, grates, and teleporters.

Adding a Teleporter

Draw a sector into the room right on the grid (Figure 3.46). This is going to become a teleporter platform. The particular specials that need to be set to make the teleporter work will be discussed later in this book.

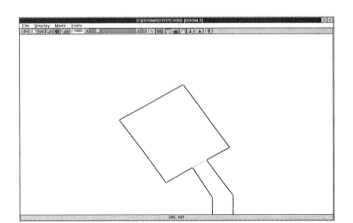

FIGURE 3.45

Drawing a room with gridlines set at 64.

F I G U R E   3 . 4 6

Drawing a sector

using the gridlines.

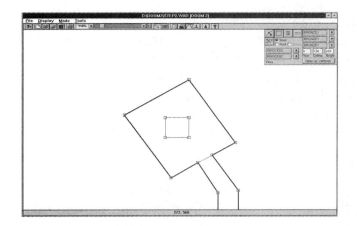

Since the teleporter must be placed precisely on the grid for the texture to line up properly, any room around the teleporter may need to be adjusted to the teleporter's position on the grid. You may want to change the shape of the room after inserting the teleporter sector, to make all of the room's texture maps conform precisely to the grid.

Hit P (Paint) and switch to Special/Texture mode. The teleporter should be raised a little above the floor and lowered a little from the ceiling to give it a more finished look. Select the teleporter sector and raise the

F I G U R E   3 . 4 7

Selecting a floor

texture from the

Flats palette.

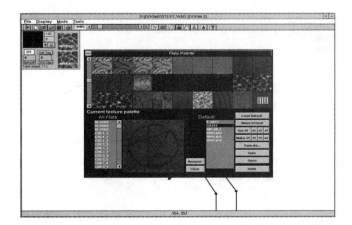

floor eight units by tapping the Ins key. Lower the ceiling by tapping the End key. (The group of keys generally found as part of the number or cursor keypad—Ins,
Del, Home, End, PgUp, and PgDn—are speed keys for
adjusting the height of the floor, the ceiling, or both.
This keyboard assignment, while nonstandard, is very
convenient for adjusting sectors. See Appendix B for a
summary of the keyboard commands.)

Appropriate flats must be picked for the floor and ceiling of the teleporter sector. Select the Flats palette icon,
and you will see the palette shown in Figure 3.47.
Scroll down until you find a texture you like for the
teleporter floor. Grab the one you want with the mouse
and drag it down to the list on the right. Drop it on the
list and it will be added to your palette (see Figure 3.48
and 3.49). Do the same for the textures you want to
use for the ceiling and the surrounding room. When
you are finished picking textures, select DONE.

Make sure the teleporter sector is selected. Get the list of
flats by selecting the arrow beside the small picture in
the upper left corner of the Sector information box.
Scroll until you see the texture you want for the sector

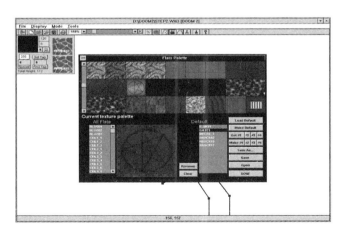

FIGURE 3.48

**Selecting a floor
texture from the
Flats palette.**

FIGURE 3.49

**The GATE3 texture
is assigned to the
floor and ceiling of
the teleporter
sector.**

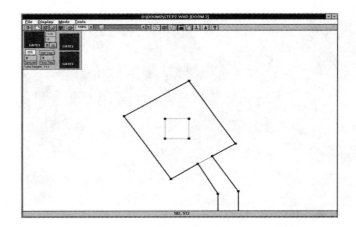

floor. Now grab the square that displays the texture and
drag it over the lower texture display. When you drop
it, the floor texture is replaced. Follow the same steps
for the ceiling texture. Then select the surrounding sector and change the floor and ceiling (Figure 3.49).

The outside of the teleporter sector has upper and
lower textures exposed. Select the outer side of any line
of the teleporter sector and you will see that all three
textures are shown in the Side information box.

Select the icon for the Wall Textures palette (Figure
3.50) and locate a suitable texture for the upper and

FIGURE 3.50

**The STEP5 texture
is selected from
the wall textures
palette.**

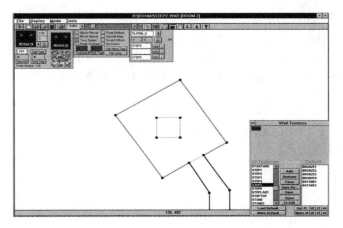

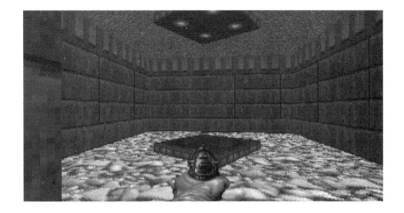

FIGURE 3.51

The teleporter is perfectly aligned to the texture as it should be.

lower portions of the sides. As you click on each texture, it will be displayed. When you find the one you want to use, make sure you have the line selected correctly and then press the Use buttons beside the top and bottom texture boxes.

Do not assign a texture to the middle box. This portion of the line is transparent (blank texture) and should not have a texture assigned to it. The "-" in the middle box indicates the blank texture, and must be present; if nothing at all is in the texture box, Doom will fail with an error.

Select the other three lines one at a time and change their textures as well. If your screen size is small and you can't see enough of the map while the Wall Textures palette is loaded, you can get it out of your way by selecting Close.

Time to take another look from Doom! Check out Figure 3.51.

Conclusion

You are now well on your way to creating your own levels. You already have seen most of the steps involved in creating the structure of a level. Later chapters will cover inserting line specials to create things like teleporters, lifts, and lighting effects.

Work on this level is continued in Chapter 5.

Testing Your Level

A semitechnical explanation of what a BSP is and how it works is given in the first part of this chapter. Note that it is not necessary for you to have any understanding of the technical details for you to be able to use the BSP. The utility itself is very simple and you can be satisfied just knowing it works.

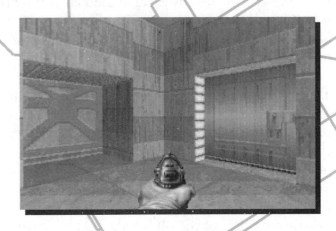

 The BSP

In a complex semi-3D environment such as Doom, program speed is of utmost importance. The BSP process allows large portions of the calculations involved to be performed ahead of time and included as part of the level data.

BSP is an acronym for Binary Space Partition. BSPs are typically used in static 3D environments with a mobile point of observation—for example, a person walking around some buildings (the buildings don't move but the viewpoint does).

The BSP is an extension of a simple z-sort. In a z-sort, all the polygons that make up a scene are sorted in order from the farthest away to the nearest, according to their Z coordinate. The polygons are then drawn onto the screen in that order. The results of this process are generally good, but the process has some problems, the worst being that it is very time consuming. The distance of every polygon center from the viewer has to be calculated each time the scene is redrawn. In the case of a high-speed action game, this can mean millions of additional computations each second.

The BSP solves this problem by creating an ordered tree of all the polygons or other objects that have to be handled. An object near the middle of the scene is chosen as the start of the tree. The position of every other object within the tree is determined by its position in 3-space relative to the object above it in the tree. In the case of objects that are not clearly on one side or the other of the object above, two virtual objects must be created that can then be placed on each side.

When the scene is displayed, you start with the first object in the tree and determine what side the viewpoint is on, then traverse down the tree on the opposite side and draw that object and continue down the tree on the side the viewpoint is on. In this way a perfect z-order is read out every time and almost instantly.

In the world of Doom, things are a bit simpler, since the map is only 2D, and it is only hundreds of sides, not thousands of polygons, that have to be dealt with.

 # How the BSP Works

In Doom the objects that are viewed as part of the structure are the SIDEDEFS. Groups of SIDEDEFS make up a displayable area. The resulting BSP tree determines the order in which to draw the walls, and the information taken from the tree is the area or sector the sides face which can be drawn.

Because it is possible to make a single sector in Doom where one wall of it might get in the way of another wall in that sector, the sectors cannot be used directly. If the sectors were used directly and one wall of the sector was in front of another from the current viewpoint, there would be no way to determine which wall was in front of the other from the tree, and the graphics might be drawn incorrectly.

To overcome this problem, any sector that is not a *convex polygon* (that is, any sector that has internal angles greater than 180) is broken up into two or more SSEC-TORS. Each SSECTOR is then one or more lines that cannot occlude each other and therefore sort to the same position in the BSP tree.

Many sectors, such as simple rectangular sectors, are already convex polygons. In these cases, the SSECTOR is the same as the SECTOR.

The SEGS define the sides of the SSECTORS much in the way that SIDEDEFS define the sides of the SEC-TORS. This means that wherever there is a two-sided line on the map, there are two SIDEDEFS and there-fore at least two SEGS.

When an SSECTOR has to be created that is different in shape from the underlying sectors, additional ver-texes are inserted into the map on lines that must be divided to participate in two more SSECTORS. This allows the line to be broken into parts so that multiple SEGS may run along it. The SEGS use existing vertexes plus the newly inserted vertexes for endpoints.

When you first load a map that has a valid BSP, you may notice these extra vertexes. You can see them by loading a map into the editor while in Special/Texture mode. When you switch to Structure mode, the editor will auto-matically clean up these extra vertexes, since they must be recalculated during the next run of the BSP.

The actual BSP routine starts by dividing the map or "world" in two somewhere near the center. An attempt is made to pick a dividing line that results in the fewest line splits. It is desirable to avoid splitting lines up into multiple SEGS, because the more splits that are creat-ed, the more SEGS and SSECTORS have to be han-dled, thus increasing processing time.

How to Use the BSP Generator

There are several command line BSP programs available for use with the Doom engine. These programs expect as input a WAD file with valid THINGS, LINEDEFS, SIDEDEFS, VERTEXES, and SECTORS. The program will generate the rest of the level data and output a new file.

There are two different BSP programs included on the disk. TBSP.EXE tends to be the faster of these, and should work fine on most systems. If you can't get TBSP to work, try BSP.EXE. Unlike BSP, TBSP does not use a 32-bit DOS extender, so it will work fine in Windows NT or Windows 95.

You must have a batch file called RUNBSP.BAT present in the directory where you save your WAD files in order for the editor to be able to BSP your levels automatically. The editor looks for this batch file and runs it. This lets you modify the settings easily, or change BSP programs simply by changing the batch file. You can also modify this batch file to do things like make a backup copy.

If you are unable to get the BSP working automatically from the editor, you can run it manually from DOS. The command line for either BSP is simply:

```
BSP infile.bsp outfile.wad
```

If you do not specify an outfile name, TMP.WAD will be created.

Occasionally you may receive an error message from the BSP program and it will abort. If the BSP program normally works for you, such an occurrence indicates something is wrong with the .WAD or .BSP file. For instance, it may contain lines that cross each other illegally, which would cause a floating point exception.

The BSP program will report the number of vertexes found, how many were used, and how many it output. A large number of new vertexes created by the BSP indicates that lots of breaks are being created due to the sector shapes.

Command Line Usage for External WADs

To load your WAD into Doom, use the -file option on the command line:

```
DOOM -FILE mylevel.wad
```

This would load the WAD file called MYLEVEL. Doom will ignore any file that does not have the .WAD file extension. Always make sure your level has passed through a BSP with no errors before running it with Doom.

To start a multiplayer game across a network, all the players must first have loaded ipx support. To load an external WAD file from the command line, enter:

```
IPXSETUP -NODES n -FILE mylevel.wad
```

where *n* is the number of players.

To play a two-player modem game with an external WAD, use the command line:

```
SERSETUP -DIAL xxxxxxx -COMn -FILE
mylevel.wad
```

where *xxxxxxx* is the number to be dialed and *n* is the number of your modem's COM port. The answering player must have exactly the same WAD file and use the command:

```
SERSETUP -ANSWER -COMx -FILE mylevel.wad
```

where COM*x* is whichever COM port your modem or serial link is on.

See the README.EXE that came with Doom or Doom II for more information on command line parameters.

 # Cheat Codes and Other Useful Options

When you are testing a level, you don't always have the time or inclination to actually play the level. To save you time, you can use these "cheat" codes while within the game:

IDSPISPOPD (Doom) Turns off the blockmap so you can walk through walls.

IDCLIP (Doom II) Same as IDSPISPOPD, but for Doom II.

IDFA Freaking Ammo: gives you all of the weapons and ammo so you can cut through the monsters faster.

IDKFA Killer Freaking Ammo: like IDFA but includes keys

When starting Doom, these may be useful on the command line:

-NOMONSTERS Turns off the monsters on the level, so you can enjoy the scenery.

-NOSOUND Turns off sound (if running Doom in a DOS session under Windows, this might be required).

Level Problems

Since Doom is so graphics intensive, you're likely to encounter some of the following errors as you begin editing your own Doom levels.

Engine Limitations and WAD Errors

If you see messed-up graphics when you enter your level, it is most likely because of an error in how the graphics were assigned, bad line attributes, or an engine limitation.

The file BADTEXT.WAD is included on the disk (see

Figure 4.1). This was created specifically to demonstrate these problems so you can learn to recognize them easily.

The **Incorrect Two-Sided** attribute for a line will cause it to look like area **A** in Figure 4.1. Any outside line (shown thick on the map display) should not have the two-sided attribute checked. If it is checked, the wall will draw incorrectly (a variation of the HOM effect). Players will not be stopped by the wall, and can pass through it into the nothingness beyond the map.

Missing Upper or Lower Textures will cause the bizarre appearance of the opening at **B**. The change in floor and ceiling heights calls for a texture to be assigned to the upper and lower texture slots of the wall, but if they are left blank, the engine will have nothing to draw in the space.

FIGURE 4.1
*Error locations
in the level
BADTEXT.WAD.*

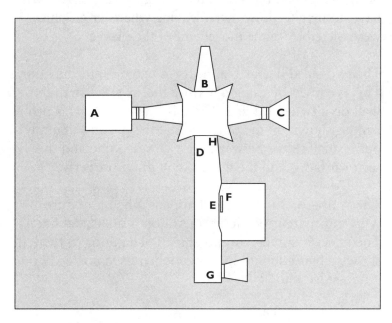

Tutti-Frutti appears when a texture is used that is shorter than the wall space it is in, or a texture with transparent areas is used on a one-sided line or an upper/lower portion of the wall. This is shown by the walls in room **C**. Portions of the texture will display properly but will be bordered on the top or bottom with colorful garbage.

The Doom engine will only repeat a wall texture vertically every 128 units. If you fill a space with a texture that is too short, it will most likely display this effect. If a texture with transparent areas is used on a wall that is one-sided (an upper or lower texture must be one-sided by definition, even if the line itself is two-sided), the engine has nothing to put in the transparent spots, and random garbage appears.

HOM (Hall Of Mirrors) is caused by missing textures on the wall, such as is shown at **D**. All one-sided walls must have a texture assigned to the normal or center portion of the SIDEDEF. If no texture is assigned, the engine will have nothing to draw there, leaving whatever graphics were there before the movement of the player.

The two-sided line at **E** appears to extend into the floor. This is caused by using a texture that is taller than the wall on a two-sided line. There is a way to fix this problem, as shown on the other side of the line at **F**. Simply put a small sector between the two-sided line and the sector it faces, and the texture will draw properly.

The wall at **G** shows what happens when a texture with transparent portions is used on a one-sided line. The effect is similar to Tutti-Frutti. The door to the left shows what it should look like when used correctly on a two-sided line.

The **Medusa Effect** is called such because your character turns to stone when you look at the wall. It is caused by incorrect normal textures on two-sided walls such as **H**. A texture assigned to a two-sided wall in the area that can be walked through must be a texture consisting of only one patch such as ASHWALL or BFALL. The Wall Texture dialog will show you the number of patches a given texture is made of.

FOB (Flash Of Black) is caused by huge changes in ceiling height. This is a limitation of the Doom engine caused by the mathematics used in calculations. If there is a difference in height of more than 1024 between the observer (player) and the area being observed, errors will occur in texture mapping. This problem has been fixed in versions of the engine 1.666 and above and is not demonstrated in BADTEXT.WAD.

Poor Texture Alignment

When using a texture that crosses multiple lines but is wider than the lines themselves, you should adjust the X offsets of the lines so that all the textures match up with each other. This gives the wall a much nicer appearance when using complex textures such as PIPES, or textures that use faces, signs, or view screens. Taking care to align textures vertically and horizontally will pay off in much nicer looking levels as well, and can be particularly effective along stairs.

Poor Texture Pegging

Textures are "pegged" to the wall space; if the wall moves, the texture moves with it. Lines have attributes that allow the wall normal or step texture to be unpegged or to "float." This prevents the texture from moving with the wall during a change in height of the sector it faces. If you forget to set this attribute, the texture will move and may look strange (although in some cases this appearance is desirable and is done deliberately). The textures in a door track are unpegged automatically by the editor if you use the automatic structure (AutoStruct) tool; in all other cases you must remember to set the appropriate attributes yourself.

Missing Player Starts

The editor will automatically warn you of this, but keep it in mind as you design the level. You should have a player start for each player in cooperative mode, as well as a minimum of four DeathMatch start locations. Usually it is better to have even more start positions on a DeathMatch level to reduce the odds of someone predicting where another player will reappear.

Line Crossing

Never allow two lines to cross each other. The crossing of two lines means the overlapping of two sectors, which cannot be handled by the Doom engine and will cause Doom to crash.

Impassable Sectors or Steps

If the difference in height between the floor and ceiling is less than 56, the player will not be able to enter the sector. Similarly, for passage from one sector to another, if the floor of the higher sector and the ceiling of the lower are too close together (less than 56), there will be insufficient space for the player to pass. See Table 3.1 for heights of other objects.

Stuck Monsters

If monsters are placed too close to each other, too close to a wall, or in a sector that is too short, they will be stuck. Players will also become stuck for the same reasons.

You can determine if an object is too close in the editor. Since the size of an object is represented accurately by its circle, any overlap with a line or another object is visible on the map display.

Bad or Missing Tags

If you accidentally tag a sector incorrectly, the LINEDEF you intended to be affected will not be, while another LINEDEF might. Far worse (but easily done!), if you leave the tag at 0 for a LINEDEF that requires a tag number, you are in effect causing that LINEDEF to affect *every* sector in the level. This can be disastrous!

Slow Game Play

Large numbers of items in a level will slow down the game. This can be a problem in multiplayer games, since the locations of all the items in the level must constantly be communicated between computers. At one time people who played DeathMatch games for hours on end in the same level were piling up tons of bodies and slowing Doom to a crawl, so early on Doom was revised to clean up dead bodies after a certain number were lying around. You still must be careful not to overdo it with monsters and objects. If you are designing your level on a decently fast machine, like a 486/66 or a Pentium, don't forget to try out your level on a slower machine once in a while. It would be wise to process the final

version of your level with the Rejects utility. See the file REJECT.TXT in REJECT11.ZIP for instructions on using the Rejects utility (on CD).

The Editing and Testing Environment

Typically, when working on a level you will switch between the editor and Doom dozens of times, perhaps every 10 minutes to half an hour.

The hardest, and most tiresome, way to do your editing is the most basic one: manually load Windows, edit your level, save it, exit to DOS, manually BSP, manually run Doom, then load Windows again. This gets annoying really fast.

Becoming efficient about how you switch between the editor and Doom will save you a great deal of time and hassle.There are several alternative setups to streamline this process, depending upon the type of computer you have. Most of these use batch files; the new Win-DOOM version of Doom makes it all even easier.

The Batch Way

The editor can be started from the DOS prompt, optionally with a filename to load automatically. This combined with the automatic exit feature when saving can reduce the amount of thinking you must do to go between Doom and editing.

Create a batch file called WORKON as follows:

```
rgdoomed d:\doom2\%1.wad
tbsp %1.bsp %1.wad

pause
doom2 -file %1.wad -wart n
dir %1.wad
pause
workon %1
```

You must include the full path to your WAD file location on the command line for the editor. The pause command after the BSP gives you a chance to break out of the batch file if there is an error. The pause after Doom gives you the same option.

The -wart option causes Doom to start up on the specified level n rather than at the opening title.

The editor will always save a .BSP file, regardless of whether you opened a .WAD or .BSP file.

On a well-optimized machine it takes only seconds to switch between editing and testing with this setup.

The Windows NT Way

If you have a Pentium class machine with 16MB of RAM and Windows NT, you have it made. Doom runs well in a DOS session on this type of machine, and you can switch between editing and testing simply by switching between windows.

For best results, use a WORKON batch file:

```
tbsp %1.bsp %1.wad
doom2 -file %1.wad -wart 1
workon %1
```

You can edit a level and save, then run this batch file. When you are finished looking at the level, hit Alt+Tab to return to the editor. Make changes and save *without running the BSP,* switch to the DOS session with Alt+Tab, press Esc, Up, Enter to quit Doom and the level you just saved with BSP, and load. Note that BSP.EXE does not work under Windows NT; you must use TBSP.EXE.

The Network Way

If you have two computers at your desk, you can edit on one while testing on the other. This is a truly ideal setup, but a bit rare. The work pattern is the same as using Windows NT, and the same basic batch file should be used.

If the two computers are running at different speeds, use the slower one for running Doom to help you catch structural problems.

The WinDOOM Way

WinDOOM (see Figure 4.2) is available only for Win32s—this means Windows NT and Windows 95. Because WinDOOM is a native Windows application, it can be switched to instantly for testing. WinDOOM was not available at the time this book was completed. Once WinDOOM is generally available, the editor will be upgraded to automatically cause WinDOOM to switch to the level just saved. This means you will be able to save the level you are working on and have Doom pop up, automatically running that level.

WinDOOM also offers superior graphics, with screens of up to 640 × 400 pixels, as compared to the DOS version, with a 320 × 200 pixel screen.

FIGURE 4.2
WinDOOM.

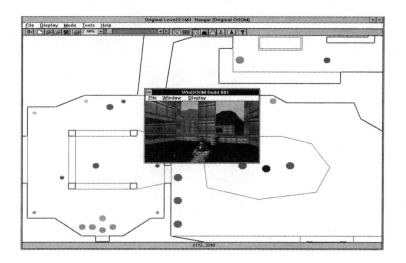

CHAPTER 5

Finishing Your Level

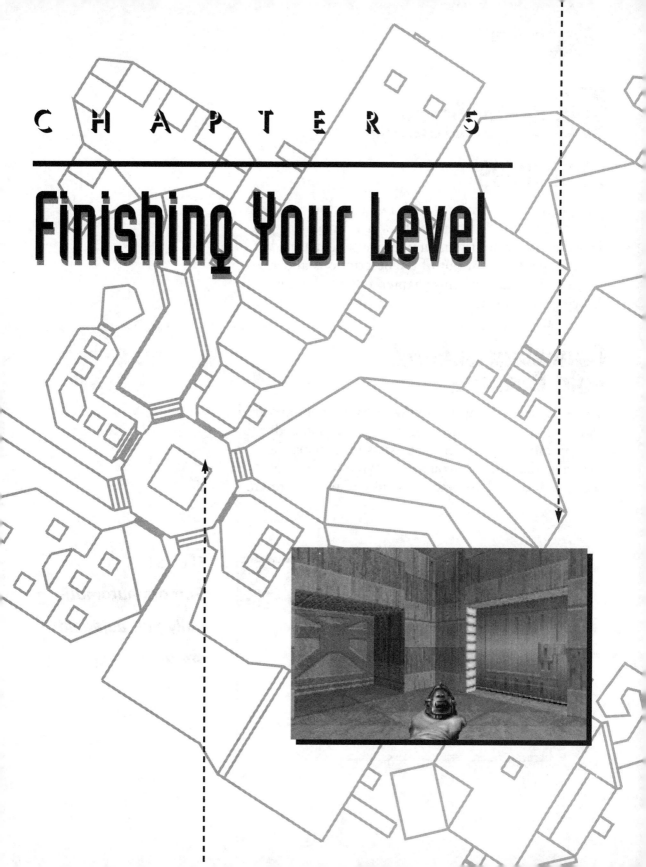

 Sector Drawing Techniques

A high level of proficiency in drawing sectors will help in creating levels. The manner in which things are drawn is important to maintaining an uncorrupted level. To get the most out of the descriptions and suggestions that make up this chapter, follow along by drawing as you read.

Canceling Sector/ Void Drawing

If you begin dragging out a new sector or void and find that your starting point is not where you intended it to be, you can easily cancel the process by moving the mouse so that the box you are drawing has a zero width or height. The sector or void will not be drawn.

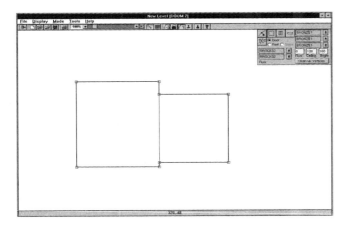

FIGURE 5.1

Sectors automatically join adjacent sectors.

Automatic Sector Joins

A new sector will automatically join itself to an existing sector if it is drawn with one of its lines close enough to the line of the other sector, the two lines are parallel, and the new line falls within the length of the existing line (see Figure 5.1). This join will occur automatically when the line is drawn left to right .

If a new sector is drawn with one or both of its ends falling outside the existing sector, then the join will not be performed automatically (Figure 5.2). This particular example can be corrected in one of two ways.

- Drag the bottom vertex from one of the two sectors to meet the other; they will become joined (Figure 5.3).

- If you want the new sector to extend below the existing sector, as drawn, insert a vertex on the line where the vertex of the existing sector should meet it (Figure 5.4). Be sure to separate the lines from each other before inserting the vertex so that the editor can determine which line you intend to break. Then drag the vertexes together manually.

FIGURE 5.2

Two adjacent sectors that are not joined (note thick center line).

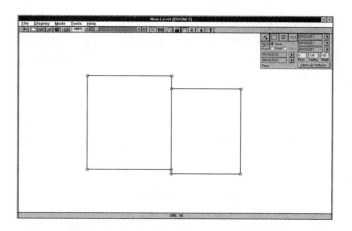

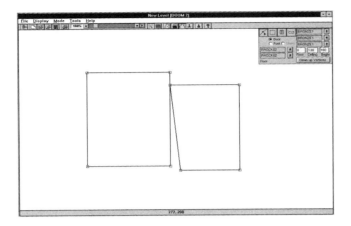

FIGURE 5.3

You can see the sectors are not joined by moving a vertex.

The sectors are now joined at an offset to each other (Figure 5.5). The procedure would be the same if both ends fell outside the first sector.

You may have two distinct sectors that are not joined in any way (Figure 5.6). To join these two sectors with a hallway, simply drag out a new sector between them (Figure 5.7). Note that you can watch the width and height of the new zone display on the status bar. The new sector is drawn precisely from line to line and joins automatically.

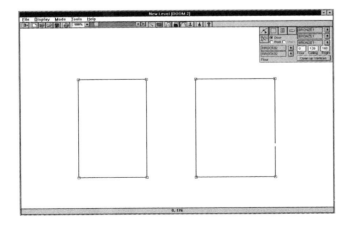

FIGURE 5.4

Make sectors meet by first inserting a new vertex.

FIGURE 5.5

*The two sectors
are joined.*

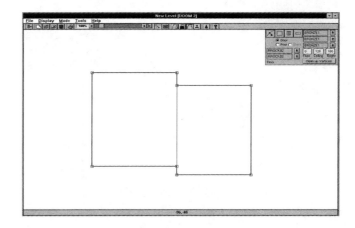

In some rare cases you will be able to draw the sector in one direction but not the other—perhaps left to right but not right to left. This is because the editor code is incorrectly identifying the action you are taking as an invalid one, and is attempting to protect you from making mistakes. Drawing in the opposite direction will allow it to see more clearly what your intention is.

Once the sectors are joined, the vertexes can be deformed as you see fit (Figure 5.8). Knock yourself out! Just remember that more complex shapes (like the

FIGURE 5.6

*Two sectors that
need a hallway
between them.*

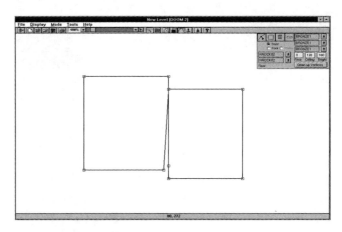

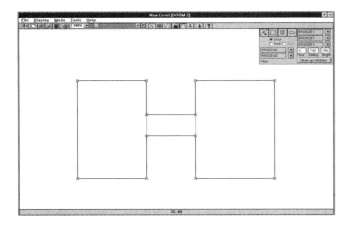

FIGURE 5.7

Adding a hallway between two adjacent sectors.

ones shown in Figure 5.9) are more demanding on the Doom engine and will slow play down somewhat. Nonconvex shapes and large numbers of two-sided lines are the most demanding.

Here is a technique for creating the same type of join but without using a sector in between. First, new vertexes are inserted on the line where vertexes from the other sector will join (Figure 5.10). Next, the vertexes are dragged and joined (Figure 5.11 and 5.12).

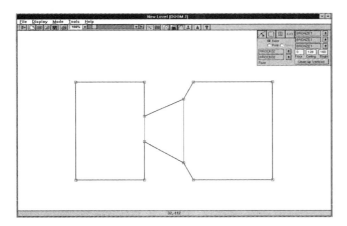

FIGURE 5.8

When sectors are joined, you can deform the vertexes to create interesting hallways.

FIGURE 5.9

Complex shapes add interest but also slow down the game.

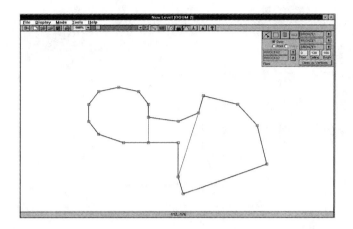

Now the two sectors connect at that narrow point. The sectors can again be deformed. You might want to insert new vertexes to return the right-hand sector to its former rectangular shape. (New vertexes could have been inserted first on the wall of the new sector facing the other sector and dragged over to connect, leaving the original four corner vertexes in place.) Or maybe you have something else in mind (Figure 5.13).

FIGURE 5.10

Add vertexes where you want the sectors to join.

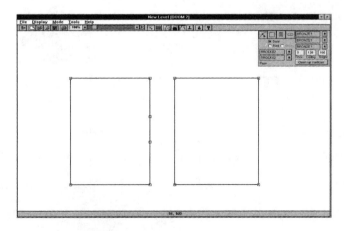

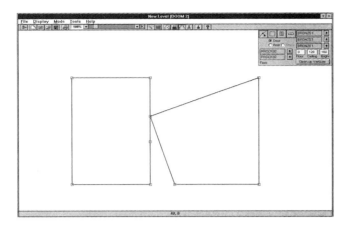

FIGURE 5.11

Drag vertexes to

join sectors.

Nested Sectors

Sectors within sectors, or *nested sectors*, are recognized automatically by the editor as they are drawn. A typical nested sector might be used to create a pool, a pedestal, a teleporter pad, or a step. A more complex object such as a boat or a couch can be built up by nesting sectors.

To create a sector inside of another, simply draw it in where you want it. Just be careful to keep the new sector entirely within its container sector (Figure 5.14).

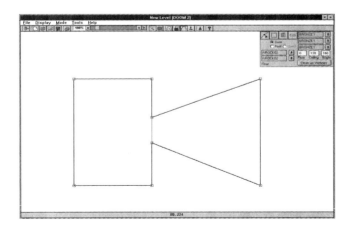

FIGURE 5.12

Sectors are now

joined.

FIGURE 5.13

You can create almost any shape by adding and deforming vertexes.

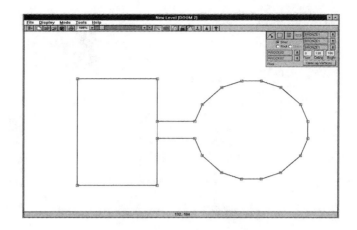

Notice that the inner sector has thin lines all around. This signifies that the lines are two-sided.

If you want a sector to be inside another but to share a common wall, the sector should be drawn attached to the wall (Figure 5.15).

Never allow a sector being drawn inside another to cross over the lines of that sector (Figure 5.16). If this happens, the newly drawn sector will cause major errors in the BSP or in Doom. *Two lines should never cross*

FIGURE 5.14

You can add sectors within sectors.

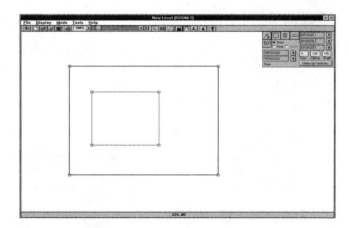

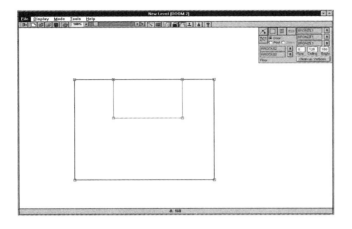

FIGURE 5.15

A nested sector that shares a wall.

each other. The only valid "crossing" of two lines is actually created with four lines joined at a single vertex.

Two-sided lines like those produced by sectors within sectors are not solid. Even though you can assign a texture to them and give them the "block player" and "block monster" attributes, they are still not considered solid by the engine for the purpose of projectiles. There is also the matter of paper-thin walls looking a bit unreal. In the situation where a solid wall is needed within a sector, a void should be used.

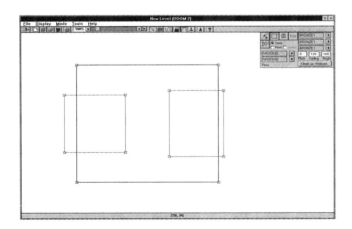

FIGURE 5.16

An improperly drawn nested sector will cause major errors in Doom.

FIGURE 5.17

FIGURE 5.17

Voids have thick lines to show they are one-sided.

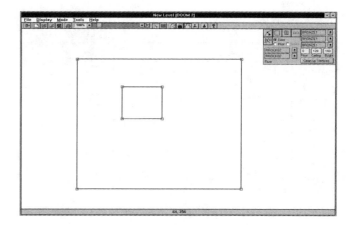

Voids and Columns

A void is simply a space within a sector, defined by lines, with no sector inside it. Voids are most typically used to create columns and so are sometimes referred to as columns.

Voids are drawn in the same manner as sectors, but using the second mouse button (see Figure 5.17). Notice that the lines defining the void appear thick to signify that they are one-sided. If you click inside the void, nothing happens, as there is no sector there to select.

FIGURE 5.18

Voids can be deformed in the same way as sectors.

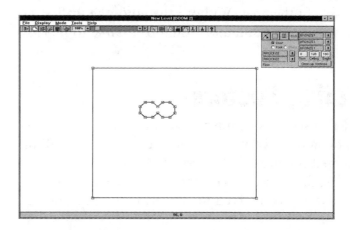

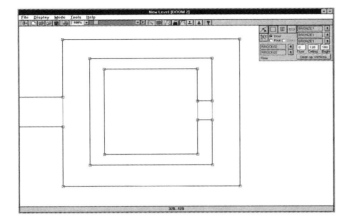

FIGURE 5.19

The wall between the inner and outer sectors is a void.

Lines defining a void can be broken, reshaped, and generally abused in the same manner as other sector lines (Figure 5.18).

There is no limit to the size of a void, as long as it is properly contained by the sector it is in. The same rule applies to voids as to sectors: *Never cross sector lines while drawing a void.*

The structure shown in Figure 5.19 is composed of a void within a sector and a sector within that void. Another sector joins the inside sector to the outside one. The void forms a solid C-shaped wall with thickness inside of the area. Without the void, the wall would seem paper thin and would be unable to block projectile weapons.

Deleting Sectors

To delete a sector, you must have the Sector tool selected. Click in the sector you want to delete and it will be highlighted (Figure 5.20). Press the D key or click on the Delete Sector icon (with the red X). Do not use the Del key, which is reserved for lowering the floor height.

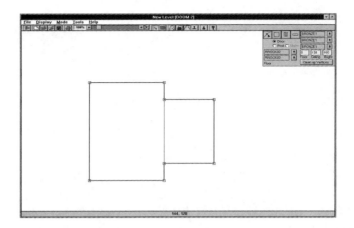

When the sector is deleted, the vertexes are left behind (Figure 5.21). This is done for two reasons: so you can see where the sector was in case you are replacing it with something else, and to make the annoyingly time-consuming job of cleaning up vertexes later on easier. To clean up the vertexes right away, click the Clean Up Vertices button.

Deleting Lines

If a sector is more complex than you want, you can selectively remove lines. This is done by moving vertexes

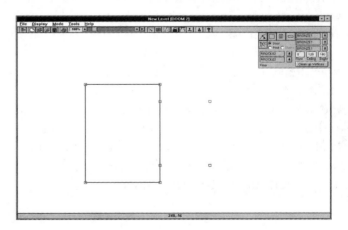

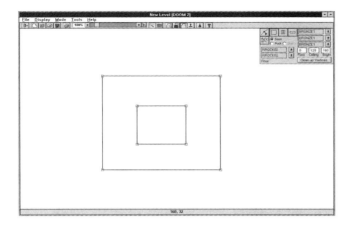

FIGURE 5.22

Deleting a nested sector leaves a void.

together. If two vertexes on either end of a line meet, the editor determines that the line is no longer needed.

Never allow a sector to be reduced to fewer than three lines.

Deleting Nested Sectors and Voids

When a nested sector is deleted, a void in the shape of the deleted sector is left behind (Figure 5.22). This void can be left or removed. If you decide to leave the void there, you must remember to remove the two-sided attribute from the lines.

To remove the void, you must delete all the lines it is made of. Start moving vertexes together, simplifying the shape, until all you have left is a line. Never leave a line like this in your map; it will cause a math failure in the BSP. Move the ends of the line together so that all you have is an orphaned vertex. The vertex can be cleaned up or left for the BSP to remove.

Line Attributes

Each line may have any of nine different attributes assigned to it. The attributes affect everything from the way in which textures are drawn to the ability the line has to block passage of objects, sight, and sound. Attributes are like switches—they are either on or off. The line attributes are listed in Table 5.1.

TABLE 5.1	Line Attributes
Attribute	**Description**
Block Player	Blocks players and monsters from going through line
Block Monster	Blocks monsters (not players) from going through line
Two Sided	Allows sight and shooting through line
Float Texture	Unlocks texture from wall space
Float Bottom	Unlocks step texture from wall space
Secret Map	Prevents display on AutoMap
Sound Block	Blocks transmission of sound
No Draw	Causes a line never to be drawn on the map
On Map	Line is already on the AutoMap at start of play

Block Player

Motion of players and monsters is blocked by a line with this attribute. This has nothing to do with being able to see through a line. For example, you might draw a window that has a window sill low enough for the player to be able to walk through the window, but wish to prevent it; to do so, use this attribute. The windows in the first room of E1M1 are blocked in this manner. Setting this attribute does *not* block shooting if the line also has the two-sided attribute set.

Although the original levels of Doom have Block Player set on all the outside walls, this was not necessary, since the game engine will not allow the player to wall though a line that does not have the two-sided attribute set.

Block Monster

Monsters cannot walk through a line with this attribute. This is mostly used to prevent monsters from doing possibly stupid things like walking off the side of a staircase or into a pit.

Two Sided

If a line has two SIDEDEFS, and both of them are completely transparent (-), then this attribute *must* be selected or the graphics for that wall will not refresh properly. Setting this attribute also allows shooting through the line even when Block Player is selected.

Be careful not to have this attribute set on a one-sided wall. If you leave it set, the wall will display the wrong texture or another graphic error which will cause Doom to slow down considerably when the wall is on the screen, even on a Pentium.

If you assign a graphic to the normal portion of a wall that is two-sided, you must take care. If you use a graphic that is made up of more than one patch, the Doom engine will be unable to display it properly and you will see what is known as the Medusa Effect: The wall texture will display as colorful garbage and Doom will slow down drastically; on many machines it will almost stop. Only single-patch textures such as ASH-WALL or BLOODWAL can be used on a two-sided line. This is due to a limitation of the Doom engine and must be lived with.

Float Texture

If this attribute is *not* selected, the texture on a wall will move up and down with the ceiling. In the case of a door frame texture (usually DOORTRAK), this attribute is set. This causes the texture to "float" at the same position on the wall and not move with the rest of the sector as its ceiling or floor height changes.

Sometimes you will want to leave this attribute off to create a special effect. One such effect is used in E1M3: There is a secret door right across from the Player 1 start location. After a bridge is raised across the acid pool, the player can reach the secret door; when it opens, the entire hallway goes up and the walls move with it.

Float Bottom

This is the same as Float Texture, but applies to the "step" texture.

Secret Map

This has nothing to do with something being secret as far as the game engine is concerned. What this

attribute does is cause the AutoMap to display secret doors as normal walls. This prevents them from being found simply by looking at the color of the map lines.

Sound Block

Despite the name of this attribute, it only blocks sound under special circumstances.

Sounds you make (such as shooting) travel to every part of the sector you are currently in, then travel into sectors that are adjacent to the sector you are in, and then to sectors adjacent to those sectors.

Sound stops in only two places: at a line that has only one side, and at boundaries between two sectors that have no overlap in their heights. This would obviously include closed doors. If the heights of the two sectors overlap at all, sound will travel between them.

If sound passes a line between sectors where sound would carry normally but the line has this attribute set, the sound level is cut by half. If the sound passes through two lines with the attribute set, the sound is blocked.

Note that the sound block attribute only affects what monsters hear, and not players. Players can always hear any sound made in a sector that has a continuous connection between them.

No Draw

This causes a line not to be drawn on the map. This attribute is generally set for lines that do not affect the real structure of the level from the player's point of view, such as a line used to separate two sectors or to create a shadow through differing brightness levels.

Line Specials and Tags

This is where 90 percent of the action in Doom level design is. Clever or not-so-clever use of line specials is what makes or breaks a level, and knowing how to make good use of them is essential. Without them you can't even have a door.

Every structure you ever see in Doom is a sector or a side of a sector. However, even though doors, stairs, and crushing ceilings are all just sectors that are behaving in different ways, you will tend to think of them as different structures. For this reason, the line specials are described by the type of desirable behavior they give you: Doors, Platforms, and so on.

You will often see the term *adjacent* used in descriptions of attributes. A sector is adjacent to another sector if they share a line. This would by definition include that very sector, so remember that every sector is adjacent to itself.

This also means that adjacent sectors do not have to literally be adjacent; one sector can actually be nested inside the other.

Some line specials—most noticeably doors and teleporters—are sensitive to the direction the line is "facing." In the case of teleporter lines, facing affects the direction in travel through a line that causes teleportation. Manual doors with the wrong line facing simply do not work. A line that faces the wrong way can just be flipped in the editor.

You can have a lot of fun experimenting with using

specials in different ways: apply a Crushing Ceiling special to a Door sector and use a Door special on an entire hallway.

Tags

All line specials, with the exception of the scrolling effect special, must be associated with a sector. All line/sector pairs must be associated with each other through use of a *tag*, except for a line special of the Manual type, which is automatically associated with the sector behind it.

A line is associated with a sector by assigning the line and sector identical tag numbers. The particular number used has no meaning (with the exception of 999, which is used in staircases). You must never leave a required tag number set to 0. Doing so will cause that line special to affect every sector on the level. This can be rather exciting, but is not what you want.

In most cases multiple sectors can be affected by the same line by using the same tag for all of them. However, in the case of teleporter sectors, having two or more destinations for one line will cause Doom to crash. You can, however, have multiple lines that teleport to a single sector.

Line Special Listing

The listing that follows contains a short description of each of the 141 line specials; the descriptions are those used in the editor. Line specials can be grouped by action activation and action type. The activations and types, which are given for each line special in the listing, are explained in Tables 5.2 and 5.3.

TABLE 5.2	Action Activations
Action Activation	**Description**
Switches	Action will occur *only once* when player presses wall. If a texture that begins with SW (switch) is used, it will be automatically animated.
Buttons	Action will occur *every time* player presses wall. If a switch texture is used, it will be automatically animated.
Manual	Activates doors that don't need a tag. The sector behind the line is the sector affected by the special.
Trigger	Action happens *only once* when the player walks over it.
ReTrigger	Action happens *every time* the player walks over it.
Impact	Shoot/punch to activate.
Effect	Used only in the case of a scrolling wall.

The specials are listed in numerical value order. The specials were created by the id level designers as needed, so the functions do not necessarily follow any pattern. There are also some different specials that are identical in behavior; in some cases, specials were created without first checking what already existed; in other cases, the same special is named in two different ways for convenience in usage. Because of the large number of activation types, there are also many specials that are very similar to one another. Table 5.4,

TABLE 5.3 Action Types

Action Type	Description
Door	Used primarily for Door type sectors. Doors that "raise" will reclose after 5 seconds. Doors that "open" will stay open.
Lift	Used primarily for Lift/Platform sectors. A lift should be built in the level at its upper height. The sector will "remember" its starting height and return to it when it comes back up. A lift always goes down to the lowest adjacent sector.
Crush	These are floors or ceilings that puree players and monsters.
Light	Creates one of many possible lighting effects in the sector.
Floor	Floors go up/down, change texture, etc. Floors that go down usually go to the *next lowest* adjacent sector.
Ceiling	Ceilings go up/down, etc.
Exit	Anything that ends a level. Note that the exit to secret level switches are only meaningful in the appropriate version of Doom.
Stairs	Related to staircases that raise from the floor automatically.
Teleport	Used for teleporting players or monsters or both.
Misc	Everything else.

which cross-references the line specials by activation and type, should prove helpful in understanding—and choosing—line specials.

All of the line specials that were in the original Doom versions 1.0–1.2 are available in all later versions of Doom. Line specials listed here as Doom II are available in all versions of the Doom engine 1.4 and higher. This includes the original Doom, provided the executable has been upgraded.

Following the name of each special in the listing is a list of the original Doom levels where this special was used [ellipses (. . .) indicate that the list is only a sampling]. To learn more about a special, you can load a level listed for that special into the editor, print the map, find the locations where the special was used, and then check it out in Doom.

Finally, there is a description of the special. In most cases it just states the definition in plain English. In a few cases there are special things you must know about using the special.

Blazing stuff (fast doors) is a special case; it can be used only with Version 1.4 and up of the Doom engine (this includes all versions of Doom II).

1

Action Activation:	Manual
Action Type:	Door
Name:	Manual_Door_Raise
Version:	Doom
Levels:	Used On: All
Description:	Opens a door, closes in 5 seconds. No tag number needed.

2

Action Activation:	Trigger
Action Type:	Door
Name:	Trigger_Open_Door
Version:	Doom
Levels:	Used on: E1M3, E1M4, E1M5..., MAP01, MAP06, MAP08...
Description:	Opens a door, stays open.

3

Action Activation:	Trigger
Action Type:	Door
Name:	Trigger_Close_Door
Version:	Doom
Levels:	Used on: E2M4, E3M2, MAP05, MAP08, MAP09, MAP13, MAP18, MAP23, MAP28
Description:	Closes a door.

4

Action Activation:	Trigger
Action Type:	Door
Name:	Trigger_Raise_Door
Version:	Doom II
Levels:	Used on: MAP10
Description:	Opens a door, closes in 5 seconds.

5

Action Activation:	Trigger
Action Type:	Floor
Name:	Trigger_Raise_Floor
Version:	Doom
Levels:	Used on: E1M4, MAP18, MAP18, MAP24
Description:	Raises floor to match adjacent floor.

6

Action Activation:	Trigger
Action Type:	Crush
Name:	Trigger_Fast_Crush_&_Raise
Version:	Doom II
Levels:	Used on: None
Description:	Starts a fast up/down crushing ceiling.

7

Action Activation:	Switch
Action Type:	Stairs
Name:	Switch_Build_Stairs
Version:	Doom
Levels:	Used on: E1M8, E2M1, E2M4, E2M5, E2M8, E3M3, MAP13, MAP18, MAP19, MAP24, MAP27
Description:	Builds a set of stairs—each step is a separate sector. Using this line special will affect three or more adjoining sectors. Each step sector will rise 8 units and trigger an adjoining step sector. The step sectors should be drawn in consecutive order, preferably from highest elevation to lowest, and must be adjacent to each other (see line specials 8, 100, and 127, and the section in this chapter "Automatic Stairs"). Each step sector should have its first side pointing out (the Doom Editor creates sectors this way by default). First step sector gets related (matching) tag number, next step no tag, third step tag number 999, then no tag, 999, and so on. Final destination sector is already at full height and is not tagged.

8

Action Activation:	Trigger
Action Type:	Stairs
Name:	Trigger_Build_Stairs
Version:	Doom
Levels:	Used on: E1M3, E2M2, MAP08
Description:	Builds a set of stairs—each step is a separate sector. Using this line special will affect three or more adjoining sectors. Each step sector will rise 8 units and trigger an adjoining step sector. The step sectors should be drawn in consecutive order, preferably from highest elevation to lowest, and must be adjacent to each other (see line specials 7, 100, and 127, and the section in this chapter "Automatic Stairs"). Each step sector should have its first side pointing out (the Doom Editor creates sectors this way by default). First step sector gets related (matching) tag number, next step no tag, third step tag number 999, then no tag, 999, and so on.. Final destination sector is already at full height and is not tagged.

9

Action Activation:	Switch
Action Type:	Floor
Name:	Switch_Change_Donut
Version:	Doom
Levels:	Used on: E1M2, E2M2
Description:	Lowers floor, raises adjacent floor, and matches outer texture.

10

Action Activation:	Trigger
Action Type:	Lift
Name:	Trigger_PlatDownWaitUpStay
Version:	Doom
Levels:	Used on: E2M2
Description:	Lowers lift (rises after 3 seconds).

11

Action Activation:	Switch
Action Type:	Exit
Name:	Switch_EXIT
Version:	Doom
Levels:	Used on: All
Description:	Exits/ends a level.

12

Action Activation:	Trigger
Action Type:	Light
Name:	Trigger_LightTurnOn
Version:	Doom II
Levels:	Used on: None
Description:	Turns light up to level of brightest adjacent sector.

13

Action Activation:	Trigger
Action Type:	Light
Name:	Trigger_LightTurnOn255
Version:	Doom
Levels:	Used on: E2M2, E2M2, E2M2, E2M2, MAP15
Description:	Turns lights to 255.

14

Action Activation:	Switch
Action Type:	Floor
Name:	Switch_RaiseFloor32
Version:	Doom
Levels:	Used on: E2M1
Description:	Raises floor 32.

15

Action Activation:	Switch
Action Type:	Floor
Name:	Switch_RaiseFloor24
Version:	Doom II
Levels:	Used on: MAP09
Description:	Raises floor 24.

16

Action Activation:	Trigger
Action Type:	Door
Name:	Trigger_CloseDoor30
Version:	Doom
Levels:	Used on: E1M6, E2M2, E2M7, MAP17, MAP23
Description:	Closes door for 30 seconds.

17

Action Activation:	Trigger
Action Type:	Light
Name:	Trigger_StartSlowStrobing
Version:	Doom
Levels:	Used on: None
Description:	Causes light to begin blinking between original light level and lowest level of an adjacent sector. If no adjacent sector has a lower brightness, it will vary between the original light level and zero.

18

Action Activation:	Switch
Action Type:	Floor
Name:	Switch_RaiseToNearestFloor
Version:	Doom
Levels:	Used on: E1M4, E3M1, E3M3, E3M4, E3M9, MAP04, MAP09, MAP12, MAP19, MAP20, MAP23, MAP29
Description:	Raises floor to nearest adjacent floor.

19

Action Activation:	Trigger
Action Type:	Floor
Name:	Trigger_LowerFloor
Version:	Doom
Levels:	Used on: E2M2, E2M4, E3M3, E3M6, MAP03, MAP06, MAP13, MAP17, MAP18, MAP19, MAP24
Description:	Lowers floor to match adjacent floor.

20	*Action Activation:*	Switch
	Action Type:	Floor
	Name:	Switch_RaiseFloorNear&Change
	Version:	Doom
	Levels:	Used on: E1M3, E1M9, E2M2..., MAP03, MAP06, MAP08
	Description:	Raises floor to nearest adjacent floor.

21	*Action Activation:*	Switch
	Action Type:	Lift
	Name:	Switch_PlatDownWaitUpStay
	Version:	Doom
	Levels:	Used on: E2M2
	Description:	Lowers floor to lowest adjacent for 3 seconds.

22	*Action Activation:*	Trigger
	Action Type:	Floor
	Name:	Trigger_RaiseFloorNear&Change
	Version:	Doom
	Levels:	Used on: E1M5, E1M7, E2M4, MAP05, MAP09, MAP12, MAP20, MAP24, MAP26
	Description:	Raises floor to match adjacent floor height, then changes texture and type to match.

23	*Action Activation:*	Switch
	Action Type:	Floor
	Name:	Switch_Lower_FloorToLowest
	Version:	Doom
	Levels:	Used on: E1M7, E1M8, E2M2..., MAP06, MAP07, MAP09...
	Description:	Lowers floor to lowest adjacent floor.

24

Action Activation:	Impact
Action Type:	Floor
Name:	Impact_RaiseFloor
Version:	Doom II
Levels:	Used on: E2M4
Description:	This LINEDEF is used to raise a floor to the ceiling (closes the sector off). It does not crush.

25

Action Activation:	Trigger
Action Type:	Crush
Name:	Trigger_CeilingCrush&Raise
Version:	Doom II
Levels:	Used on: None
Description:	Starts an up/down crushing ceiling.

26

Action Activation:	Manual
Action Type:	Door
Name:	Manual_Door_Raise_Blue
Version:	Doom
Levels:	Used on: E1M3, E1M4, E1M5..., MAP03, MAP11, MAP12...
Description:	Opens a blue door (closes after 5 seconds).

27

Action Activation:	Manual
Action Type:	Door
Name:	Manual_Door_Raise_Yellow
Version:	Doom
Levels:	Used on: E1M3, E1M4, E1M5..., MAP10, MAP12, MAP15...
Description:	Opens a yellow door (closes after 5 seconds).

28

Action Activation:	Manual
Action Type:	Door
Name:	Manual_Door_Raise_Red
Version:	Doom
Levels:	Used on: E1M2, E1M6, E1M7, E2M1, MAP05, MAP11, MAP24, MAP27
Description:	Opens a red door (closes after 5 seconds).

29

Action Activation:	Switch
Action Type:	Door
Name:	Switch_Raise_Door
Version:	Doom
Levels:	Used on: E2M1
Description:	Opens a door (closes after 5 seconds).

30

Action Activation:	Trigger
Action Type:	Floor
Name:	Trigger_RaiseToShortTexture
Version:	Doom
Levels:	Used on: E2M2, E3M2, MAP15, MAP17
Description:	Raises floor to 64 above adjacent floor.

31

Action Activation:	Manual
Action Type:	Door
Name:	Manual_Door_Open
Version:	Doom
Levels:	Used on: E1M2, E1M3, E1M4..., MAP01, MAP07, MAP08...
Description:	Opens a door (stays open).

32

Action Activation:	Manual
Action Type:	Door
Name:	Manual_Door_Open_Blue
Version:	Doom
Levels:	Used on: E1M9, E2M2, E2M4..., MAP02, MAP05, MAP06...
Description:	Opens a blue door (stays open).

33

Action Activation:	Manual
Action Type:	Door
Name:	Manual_Door_Open_Red
Version:	Doom
Levels:	Used on: E1M9, E2M2, E2M6..., MAP03, MAP06, MAP08...
Description:	Opens a red door (stays open).

34

Action Activation:	Manual
Action Type:	Door
Name:	Manual_Door_Open_Yellow
Version:	Doom
Levels:	Used on: E1M7, E1M9, E2M4..., MAP05, MAP08, MAP09...
Description:	Opens a yellow door (stays open).

35

Action Activation:	Trigger
Action Type:	Light
Name:	Trigger_Lights_Very_Dark
Version:	Doom
Levels:	Used on: E1M3, MAP15, MAP18, MAP24, MAP26, MAP27, MAP28
Description:	Brightness goes to 0.

36

Action Activation:	Trigger
Action Type:	Floor
Name:	Trigger_Turbo_Lower_Floor
Version:	Doom
Levels:	Used on: E1M1, E1M4, E1M6, E1M9, E2M1, E2M5, E3M2, MAP12, MAP13, MAP18, MAP19, MAP20, MAP21, MAP24, MAP27, MAP28
Description:	Lowers floor to floor level of adjacent sector.

37

Action Activation:	Trigger
Action Type:	Floor
Name:	Trigger_LowerFloor&Change
Version:	Doom
Levels:	Used on: E2M1, E2M6, E3M1..., MAP08, MAP12, MAP26
Description:	Lowers floor to match adjacent floor, matches texture and type.

38

Action Activation:	Trigger
Action Type:	Floor
Name:	Trigger_Lower_Floor_To_Lowest
Version:	Doom
Levels:	Used on: E2M2, E3M2, E3M5, E3M6, E3M9, MAP07, MAP08, MAP09...
Description:	Lowers floor to match adjacent floor.

39

Action Activation:	Trigger
Action Type:	Teleport
Name:	Trigger_TELEPORT
Version:	Doom
Levels:	Used on: E3M6, E3M9, MAP12, MAP19, MAP27
Description:	Teleports to another sector.

40

Action Activation:	Trigger
Action Type:	Misc
Name:	Trigger_LowerFloorRaiseCeiling
Version:	Doom
Levels:	Used on: E3M5
Description:	Raises ceiling to adjacent ceiling.

41

Action Activation:	Switch
Action Type:	Ceiling
Name:	Switch_Lower_Ceiling_To_Floor
Version:	Doom
Levels:	Used on: None
Description:	Lowers ceiling to floor.

42

Action Activation:	Button
Action Type:	Door
Name:	Button_Close_Door
Version:	Doom
Levels:	Used on: E3M1, E3M9, MAP14
Description:	Closes a door.

43

Action Activation:	Button
Action Type:	Ceiling
Name:	Button_Lower_Ceiling_To_Floor
Version:	Doom II
Levels:	Used on: None
Description:	Lowers the ceiling to the floor.

44

Action Activation:	Trigger
Action Type:	Crush
Name:	Trigger_Ceiling_Crush
Version:	Doom
Levels:	Used on: E3M5
Description:	Lowers ceiling to 8 above floor and crushes.

45

Action Activation:	Button
Action Type:	Floor
Name:	Button_Lower_Floor
Version:	Doom II
Levels:	Used on: MAP18
Description:	Lowers floor to next lowest adjacent floor height.

46

Action Activation:	Impact
Action Type:	Door
Name:	Impact_OpenDoor
Version:	Doom
Levels:	Used on: E1M2, E2M4, E3M2, MAP08, MAP10, MAP16, MAP18, MAP20, MAP23, MAP27, MAP28
Description:	Opens a door when line is shot (stays open).

47

Action Activation:	Impact
Action Type:	Floor
Name:	Impact_RaiseFloorNear&Change
Version:	Doom II
Levels:	Used on: MAP19
Description:	When floor is shot, raises floor to the nearest adjacent floor and changes floor texture to match that floor.

48

Action Activation:	Effect
Action Type:	Misc
Name:	Effect_Firstcol_Scroll
Version:	Doom
Levels:	Used on: Lots
Description:	Causes the wall graphics to start scrolling. Needs no tag, always in effect.

49

Action Activation:	Switch
Action Type:	Crush
Name:	Switch_CeilingCrush&Raise
Version:	Doom II
Levels:	Used on: MAP06
Description:	Causes a crush and raises ceiling.

50

Action Activation:	Switch
Action Type:	Door
Name:	Switch_Close_Door
Version:	Doom II
Levels:	Used on: None
Description:	Closes a door.

51

Action Activation:	Switch
Action Type:	Exit
Name:	Switch_SecretExit
Version:	Doom
Levels:	Used on: E1M3, E2M5, E3M6, MAP31
Description:	Exits to secret area ExM9 or MAP32.

52

Action Activation:	Trigger
Action Type:	Exit
Name:	Trigger_EXIT
Version:	Doom
Levels:	Used on: E2M9, E3M1, E3M2, MAP12, MAP13, MAP15
Description:	Ends/exits level.

53

Action Activation:	Trigger
Action Type:	Lift
Name:	Trigger_PerpetualPlatformRaise
Version:	Doom II
Levels:	Used on: None
Description:	Platform goes down to lowest adjacent sector, then back up, then back down, and so forth.

54

Action Activation:	Trigger
Action Type:	Lift
Name:	Trigger_PlatformStop
Version:	Doom II
Levels:	Used on: None
Description:	Stops a platform (created with 53) from going up and down.

55

Action Activation:	Switch
Action Type:	Crush
Name:	Switch_Raise_FloorCrush
Version:	Doom II
Levels:	Used on: None
Description:	Raises floor to 8 below ceiling and crushes. Redecorates in Arterial Red.

56

Action Activation:	Trigger
Action Type:	Crush
Name:	Trigger_Raise_FloorCrush
Version:	Doom
Levels:	Used on: E2M4, E3M6
Description:	Raises floor to 8 below ceiling and crushes.

57

Action Activation:	Trigger
Action Type:	Crush
Name:	Trigger_CeilingCrushStop
Version:	Doom II
Levels:	Used on: None
Description:	Stops ceiling crush.

58

Action Activation:	Trigger
Action Type:	Floor
Name:	Trigger_Raise_Floor_24
Version:	Doom
Levels:	Used on: E2M4
Description:	Raises floor 24.

59

Action Activation:	Trigger
Action Type:	Floor
Name:	Trigger_Raise_Floor_24&Change
Version:	Doom
Levels:	Used on: E2M2, MAP12
Description:	Raises floor 24 and matches adjacent texture and type.

60

Action Activation:	Button
Action Type:	Floor
Name:	Button_Lower_Floor_To_Lowest
Version:	Doom II
Levels:	Used on: MAP14, MAP25, MAP27
Description:	Lowers floor to the lowest adjacent floor height.

61

Action Activation:	Button
Action Type:	Door
Name:	Button_Open_Door
Version:	Doom
Levels:	Used on: E2M6, E3M1, E3M4..., MAP06, MAP08, MAP09...
Description:	Opens a door.

62

Action Activation:	Button
Action Type:	Lift
Name:	Button_Plat_Down_Wait_Up_Stay
Version:	Doom
Levels:	Used on: E1M2, E1M3, E1M4..., MAP01, MAP05, MAP06...
Description:	Lowers a lift (also, retriggers to raise a lift).

63

Action Activation:	Button
Action Type:	Door
Name:	Button_Raise_Door
Version:	Doom
Levels:	Used on: E1M3, E1M7, E2M1..., MAP09, MAP10, MAP14...
Description:	Opens a door (closes after 5 seconds).

64

Action Activation:	Button
Action Type:	Floor
Name:	Button_Raise_Floor
Version:	Doom II
Levels:	Used on: None
Description:	This LINEDEF raises a floor to the ceiling.

65

Action Activation:	Button
Action Type:	Crush
Name:	Button_Raise_Floor_Crush
Version:	Doom II
Levels:	Used on: None
Description:	Raises a floor to the ceiling and crushes the player/monster.

66

Action Activation:	Button
Action Type:	Floor
Name:	Button_Raise_Floor_24
Version:	Doom II
Levels:	Used on: None
Description:	Raises a floor 24.

67

Action Activation:	Button
Action Type:	Floor
Name:	Button_Raise_Floor_32
Version:	Doom II
Levels:	Used on: MAP19, MAP24
Description:	Raises a floor 32.

68

Action Activation:	Button
Action Type:	Floor
Name:	Button_Raise_Floor_Near&Change
Version:	Doom II
Levels:	Used on: MAP19, MAP22
Description:	Raises floor height to match the floor height of the next highest adjacent sector. Also changes floor texture and type to match the values of that adjacent sector.

69

Action Activation:	Button
Action Type:	Floor
Name:	Button_Raise_To_Nearest_Floor
Version:	Doom II
Levels:	Used on: None
Description:	Raises a floor to the level of the next higher adjacent floor.

70

Action Activation:	Button
Action Type:	Floor
Name:	Button_Turbo_Lower_Floor
Version:	Doom
Levels:	Used on: E1M5, E1M5, E1M7, MAP20, MAP28
Description:	This button lowers a floor very fast to 8 above next lower adjacent floor.

71

Action Activation:	Switch
Action Type:	Floor
Name:	Switch_Turbo_Lower_Floor
Version:	Doom II
Levels:	MAP07, MAP10, MAP12...
Description:	Lowers a floor fast.

72

Action Activation:	Retrigger
Action Type:	Crush
Name:	Retrigger_Ceiling_Crush
Version:	Doom II
Levels:	Used on: None
Description:	Start a crushing ceiling.

73

Action Activation:	Retrigger
Action Type:	Crush
Name:	Retrigger_Ceiling_Crush_&_Raise
Version:	Doom
Levels:	Used on: E2M2, E2M4, E2M6, E3M4, E3M5, MAP13, MAP14, MAP19
Description:	Starts an up/down crushing ceiling.

74

Action Activation:	Retrigger
Action Type:	Crush
Name:	Retrigger_Ceiling_Crush_Stop
Version:	Doom
Levels:	Used on: E2M2, E2M4, E2M6, E3M4, E3M5, MAP06, MAP13, MAP14, MAP19
Description:	Stops a crushing ceiling.

75

Action Activation:	Retrigger
Action Type:	Door
Name:	Retrigger_Close_Door
Version:	Doom
Levels:	Used on: E2M8, E3M4, E3M6
Description:	Closes a door.

76

Action Activation:	Retrigger
Action Type:	Door
Name:	Retrigger_Close_Door_30
Version:	Doom
Levels:	Used on: E1M6
Description:	Closes a door for 30 seconds, then opens it.

77

Action Activation:	Retrigger
Action Type:	Crush
Name:	Retrigger_Fast_Crush_&_Raise
Version:	Doom
Levels:	Used on: E2M2, E2M4, MAP13
Description:	Causes a fast crush ceiling.

78

Action Activation:	Retrigger
Action Type:	Light
Name:	Retrigger_LightsToDimmestNear
Version:	Doom II
Levels:	Used on: None
Description:	Lowers light level to lowest adjacent level.

79

Action Activation:	Retrigger
Action Type:	Light
Name:	Retrigger_Lights_Very_Dark
Version:	Doom II
Levels:	Used on: None
Description:	Lowers light level to 0.

80

Action Activation:	Retrigger
Action Type:	Light
Name:	Retrigger_Light_Turn_On
Version:	Doom
Levels:	Used on: None
Description:	Turns the lights on to maximum adjacent light level.

81

Action Activation:	Retrigger
Action Type:	Light
Name:	Retrigger_Light_Turn_On_255
Version:	Doom II
Levels:	Used on: None
Description:	Turns the brightness of sector to 255.

82

Action Activation:	Retrigger
Action Type:	Floor
Name:	Retrigger_Lower_Floor_To_Lowest
Version:	Doom
Levels:	Used on: E1M8, E3M5, E3M6
Description:	Lowers floor to lowest adjacent floor.

83

Action Activation:	Retrigger
Action Type:	Floor
Name:	Retrigger_Lower_Floor
Version:	Doom II
Levels:	Used on: MAP13, MAP20
Description:	Lowers floor to next lower adjacent sector.

84

Action Activation:	Retrigger
Action Type:	Floor
Name:	Retrigger_Lower_Floor_&_Change
Version:	Doom II
Levels:	Used on: None
Description:	Lowers floor to next lower floor and changes to that floor texture.

85

Action Activation:	Retrigger
Action Type:	Misc
Name:	Retrigger_LwrFloorRaiseCeiling
Version:	Used on: None
Levels:	Doom II
Description:	This LINEDEF does nothing!

86

Action Activation:	Retrigger
Action Type:	Door
Name:	Retrigger_Open_Door
Version:	Doom
Levels:	Used on: E1M4, E2M8, E3M4, MAP05, MAP09, MAP29
Description:	Opens a door (stays open).

87

Action Activation:	Retrigger
Action Type:	Lift
Name:	Retrigger_Perpetual_Plat_Raise
Version:	Doom2
Levels:	E2M2, E2M3, MAP12, MAP13, MAP19
Description:	See previous.

88

Action Activation:	Retrigger
Action Type:	Lift
Name:	Retrigger_PlatDownWaitUpStay
Version:	Doom
Levels:	Used on: Lots
Description:	Lowers a platform, waits 3 seconds, then raises it back to starting point.

89

Action Activation:	Retrigger
Action Type:	Lift
Name:	Retrigger_Platform_Stop
Version:	Doom
Levels:	Used on: E2M2, E2M3, MAP12, MAP13, MAP19
Description:	Stops a moving floor.

90

Action Activation:	Retrigger
Action Type:	Door
Name:	Retrigger_Raise_Door
Version:	Doom
Levels:	Used on: E1M3, E1M4, E1M5, E1M7, E1M9, E3M5, MAP10, MAP19, MAP20, MAP26
Description:	Opens a door (closes after 5 seconds).

91

Action Activation:	Retrigger
Action Type:	Floor
Name:	Retrigger_Raise_Floor
Version:	Doom
Levels:	Used on: E1M5, E1M7, E1M8, MAP20
Description:	Raises a floor to match adjacent ceiling.

92

Action Activation:	Retrigger
Action Type:	Floor
Name:	Retrigger_Raise_Floor_24
Version:	Doom II
Levels:	Used on: None
Description:	Raises a floor 24.

93

Action Activation:	Retrigger
Action Type:	Floor
Name:	Retrigger_RaiseFloor24_&_Change
Version:	Doom II
Levels:	Used on: None
Description:	Raises floor 24 and changes floor texture to adjacent sector texture and special value.

94

Action Activation:	Retrigger
Action Type:	Crush
Name:	Retrigger_Raise_Floor_Crush
Version:	Doom II
Levels:	Used on: MAP20
Description:	Raises floor to ceiling and crushes.

95

Action Activation:	Retrigger
Action Type:	Floor
Name:	Retrigger_RaiseFloorNear&Change
Version:	Doom II
Levels:	Used on: None
Description:	Raises floor to next higher adjacent floor and changes texture to match.

96

Action Activation:	Retrigger
Action Type:	Misc
Name:	Retrigger_Raise_ToShortTexture
Version:	Used on: None
Levels:	Doom II
Description:	Raises sector by the hight of the shortest texture facing outward from the sector; every time player walks across it, raises it that much more. The ceiling will not move, but the floor will keep getting higher regardless of ceiling height. This will look strange because of the appearance of the side textures when the floor goes above the ceiling.

97

Action Activation:	Retrigger
Action Type:	Teleport
Name:	Retrigger_TELEPORT
Version:	Doom
Levels:	Used on: Lots
Description:	Causes a teleport; you must have a teleport landing pad (a THING) in the sector you teleport to. The direction that the teleport landing pad faces determines the direction the player faces upon teleport and is set just like the facing of a monster or player. There can be multiple lines per pad, but only one pad per line; game crashes if there is more than one teleport to the same spot for a single line.

98

Action Activation:	Retrigger
Action Type:	Floor
Name:	Retrigger_Turbo_Lower_Floor
Version:	Doom II
Levels:	Used on: E1M5, E1M7
Description:	Lowers floor fast.

99

Action Activation:	Button
Action Type:	Door
Name:	Button_BlzOpenDoor_Blue
Version:	Doom II
Levels:	Used on: MAP04
Description:	Quickly opens a blue door sector (stays open).

100

Action Activation:	Trigger
Action Type:	Stairs
Name:	Trigger_BuildStairsTurbo16
Version:	Doom II
Levels:	Used on: MAP09
Description:	Builds a set of stairs—each step is a separate sector. Using this line special will affect three or more adjoining sectors. Each step sector will rise 16 units quickly and trigger an adjoining step sector. The step sectors should be drawn in consecutive order, preferably from highest elevation to lowest, and must be adjacent to each other (see line specials 7, 8, and 127, and the section in this chapter "Automatic Stairs"). Each step sector should have its first side pointing out (the Doom Editor creates sectors this way by default). First step sector gets related (matching) tag number, next step no tag, third step tag number 999, then no tag, 999, and so on. Final destination sector is already at full height and is not tagged.

101

Action Activation:	Switch
Action Type:	Floor
Name:	Switch_Raise_Floor
Version:	Doom II
Levels:	Used on: None
Description:	Raises a floor.

102

Action Activation:	Switch
Action Type:	Floor
Name:	Switch_Lower_Floor
Version:	Doom
Levels:	Used on: E2M1, E2M2, E2M4..., MAP01, MAP02, MAP04...
Description:	Lowers floor to match next lowest adjacent floor.

103

Action Activation:	Switch
Action Type:	Door
Name:	Switch_Open_Door
Version:	Doom
Levels:	Used on: E1M2, E1M3, E1M5..., MAP01, MAP03, MAP05...
Description:	Opens a door (stays open).

104

Action Activation:	Trigger
Action Type:	Light
Name:	Trigger_Lights_To_Dimmest_Near
Version:	Doom
Levels:	Used on: E2M5, E3M9
Description:	Lowers light level to minimum adjacent light level.

105

Action Activation:	Retrigger
Action Type:	Door
Name:	Retrigger_Blazing_Door_Raise
Version:	Doom II
Levels:	Used on: MAP11, MAP14, MAP15, MAP17, MAP25, MAP26
Description:	Opens a door very fast (closes after 5 seconds).

106

Action Activation:	Retrigger
Action Type:	Door
Name:	Retrigger_Blazing_Door_Open
Version:	Doom II
Levels:	Used on: MAP05, MAP15, MAP16
Description:	Opens a door very fast (stays open).

107

Action Activation:	Retrigger
Action Type:	Door
Name:	Retrigger_Blazing_Door_Close
Version:	Doom II
Levels:	Used on: None
Description:	Closes a door very fast.

108

Action Activation:	Trigger
Action Type:	Door
Name:	Trigger_Blazing_Door_Raise
Version:	Doom II
Levels:	Used on: None
Description:	Opens a door very fast (closes after 5 seconds).

109

Action Activation:	Trigger
Action Type:	Door
Name:	Trigger_Blazing_Door_Open
Version:	Doom II
Levels:	Used on: MAP02, MAP03, MAP04
Description:	Opens a door very fast (stays open).

110

Action Activation:	Trigger
Action Type:	Door
Name:	Trigger_Blazing_Door_Close
Version:	Doom II
Levels:	Used on: MAP27
Description:	Closes a door very fast.

111

Action Activation:	Switch
Action Type:	Door
Name:	Switch_Blazing_Door_Raise
Version:	Doom II
Description:	Opens a door very fast (closes after 5 seconds).

112

Action Activation:	Switch
Action Type:	Door
Name:	Switch_Blazing_Door_Open
Version:	Doom II
Levels:	Used on: MAP09, MAP17, MAP27
Description:	Opens a door very fast (stays open).

113	*Action Activation:*	Switch
	Action Type:	Door
	Name:	Switch_Blazing_Door_Close
	Version:	Doom II
	Levels:	Used on: None
	Description:	Closes a door very fast.

114	*Action Activation:*	Button
	Action Type:	Door
	Name:	Button_Blazing_Door_Raise
	Version:	Doom II
	Levels:	Used on: MAP02, MAP03, MAP04...
	Description:	Opens a door very fast (closes after 5 seconds).

115	*Action Activation:*	Button
	Action Type:	Door
	Name:	Button_Blazing_Door_Open
	Version:	Doom II
	Levels:	Used on: MAP05, MAP06, MAP26, MAP27
	Description:	Quickly opens a door (stays open).

116	*Action Activation:*	Button
	Action Type:	Door
	Name:	Button_Blazing_Door_Close
	Version:	Doom II
	Levels:	Used on: MAP26
	Description:	Quickly closes a door.

117	*Action Activation:*	Manual
	Action Type:	Door
	Name:	Manual_Blazing_Door_Raise
	Version:	Doom II
	Levels:	Used on: MAP02, MAP05, MAP06...
	Description:	Opens a door very fast (closes after 5 seconds).

118

Action Activation:	Manual
Action Type:	Door
Name:	Manual_Blazing_Door_Open
Version:	Doom II
Levels:	Used on: MAP17, MAP22, MAP23...
Description:	Opens a door very fast (stays open).

119

Action Activation:	Trigger
Action Type:	Floor
Name:	Trigger_RaiseToNearestFloor
Version:	Doom II
Levels:	Used on: MAP12, MAP15, MAP26, MAP28, MAP29
Description:	Raises floor to next higher adjacent floor height.

120

Action Activation:	Retrigger
Action Type:	Lift
Name:	Retrigger_BlazeDownWaitUpStay
Version:	Doom II
Levels:	Used on: MAP03, MAP05, MAP06
Description:	Lowers a platform very fast, waits 3 seconds, and returns the platform to the original height.

121

Action Activation:	Trigger
Action Type:	Lift
Name:	Trigger_BlazeDownWaitUpStay
Version:	Doom II
Levels:	Used on: None
Description:	Lowers a platform fast, waits 3 seconds, and returns it to original height.

122

Action Activation:	Switch
Action Type:	Lift
Name:	Switch_BlazeDownWaitUpStay
Version:	Doom II
Levels:	Used on: None
Description:	Lowers a platform fast, waits 3 seconds, and returns it to starting height.

123

Action Activation:	Button
Action Type:	Lift
Name:	Button_BlazeDownWaitUpStay
Version:	Doom
Levels:	Used on: MAP03, MAP05, MAP06...
Description:	Quickly lowers a sector to the next lower adjacent sector, waits 3 seconds, and returns sector to original level.

124

Action Activation:	Trigger
Action Type:	Exit
Name:	Trigger_SecretEXIT
Version:	Doom II
Levels:	Used on: MAP15
Description:	Exit to secret level 31. No effect in Doom.

125

Action Activation:	Trigger
Action Type:	Teleport
Name:	Trigger_TELEPORT_MonsterONLY
Version:	Doom II
Levels:	Used on: MAP08
Description:	Causes monsters that cross this linedef to teleport to tagged sector. Doesn't affect players.

126

Action Activation:	Retrigger
Action Type:	Teleport
Name:	Retrigger_TELEPORT_MonsterONLY
Version:	Doom II
Levels:	Used on: MAP10, MAP16, MAP20, MAP29
Description:	Causes monsters that cross this LINEDEF to teleport to tagged sector. Doesn't affect players.

127

Action Activation:	Switch
Action Type:	Stairs
Name:	Switch_BuildStairsTurbo16
Version:	Doom II
Levels:	Used on: MAP15, MAP21
Description:	Builds a set of stairs—each step is a separate sector. Using this line special will affect three or more adjoining sectors. Each step sector will rise 16 units fast and trigger an adjoining step sector. The step sectors should be drawn in consecutive order, preferably from highest elevation to lowest, and must be adjacent to each other (see line specials 7, 8, and 100, and the section in this chapter "Automatic Stairs"). Each step sector should have its first side pointing out (the Doom Editor creates sectors this way by default). First step sector gets related (matching) tag number, next step no tag, third step tag number 999, then no tag, 999, and so on. Final destination sector is already at full height and is not tagged.

128

Action Activation:	Retrigger
Action Type:	Floor
Name:	Retrigger_RaiseToNearestFloor
Version:	Doom II
Levels:	Used on: None
Description:	Raises floor to next higher adjacent floor height.

129

Action Activation:	Retrigger
Action Type:	Crush
Name:	Retrigger_Raise_Floor_Turbo
Version:	Doom II
Levels:	Used on: None
Description:	Raises floor fast and crushes. Ouch.

130

Action Activation:	Trigger
Action Type:	Floor
Name:	Trigger_Raise_Floor_Turbo
Version:	Doom II
Levels:	Used on: None
Description:	Raises a floor fast.

131

Action Activation:	Switch
Action Type:	Floor
Name:	Switch_Raise_Floor_Turbo
Version:	Doom II
Levels:	Used on: MAP29
Description:	Raises a floor fast.

132

Action Activation:	Button
Action Type:	Floor
Name:	Button_Raise_Floor_Turbo
Version:	Doom II
Levels:	Used on: None
Description:	Raises a floor very fast up to next higher adjacent floor.

133

Action Activation:	Switch
Action Type:	Door
Name:	Switch_BlzOpenDoor_Blue
Version:	Doom II
Description:	Opens a blue door very fast (stays open)

134

Action Activation:	Button
Action Type:	Door
Name:	Button_BlzOpenDoor_Red
Version:	Doom II
Levels:	Used on: MAP04
Description:	LINEDEF quickly opens a red door sector (stays open).

135

Action Activation:	Switch
Action Type:	Door
Name:	Switch_BlzOpenDoor_Red
Version:	Doom II
Levels:	Used on: MAP02
Description:	Opens a red door very fast (stays open).

136

Action Activation:	Button
Name:	Button_BlzOpenDoor_Yellow
Version:	Doom II
Levels:	Used on: MAP04, MAP06
Description:	LINEDEF quickly opens a yellow door sector (stays open).

137

Action Activation:	Switch
Action Type:	Door
Name:	Switch_BlzOpenDoor_Yellow
Version:	Doom II
Levels:	Used on: MAP15
Description:	Opens a yellow door very fast (stays open).

138

Action Activation:	Button
Action Type:	Light
Name:	Button_Light_TurnOn
Version:	Doom II
Levels:	Used on: MAP04, MAP28
Description:	This LINEDEF is used to turn the light level of a sector on.

139

Action Activation:	Button
Action Type:	Light
Name:	Button_Light_TurnOff
Version:	Doom II
Levels:	Used on: MAP04, MAP28
Description:	This LINEDEF turns the light level of a sector off.

140

Action Activation:	Switch
Action Type:	Floor
Name:	Switch_RaiseFloor512
Version:	Doom II
Levels:	Used on: MAP30
Description:	Raises floor 512.

141

Action Activation:	Trigger
Action Type:	Crush
Name:	Trigger_SilentCeilCrush&Raise
Version:	Doom II
Levels:	Used on: MAP04
Description:	Stealthly crushing ceiling. Nasty!

TABLE 5.4	Line Special Cross Index		
	Switch	**Button**	**Manual**
Door	29, 50, 103, 111, 112, 113, 133, 135, 137	42, 61, 63, 99, 114, 115, 116, 134, 136	1, 26, 27, 28, 31, 32, 33, 34, 117, 118
Lift	21, 122	62, 123	
Crush	49, 55	65	
Light		138, 139	
Floor	9, 14, 15, 18, 20, 23, 71, 101, 102, 131, 140	45, 60, 64, 66, 67, 68, 69, 90, 132	
Ceiling	41	43	
Exit	11, 51		
Stairs	7, 127		
Teleport			

 # Automatic Stairs

Automatic stairs appear flush to the floor when you first enter a Doom level. After the stairs are activated by a line special, they raise up. Look at the original Doom levels listed with the relevant line specials for examples.

All the steps of an automatic staircase begin at floor level except for the highest step. The building of automatic stairs is started with a line special that acts on the first step sector. That sector has a tag matching the line that activates it. The next step has a tag of zero, and the following step has a tag of 999. Step sectors follow this alternating pattern of tags until the last step that moves, which can have a tag of 999 or 0. The sector

Trigger	Retrigger	Impact
2, 3, 4, 16, 108, 109, 110	75, 76, 86, 90, 105, 106, 107	46
10, 53, 54, 121	87, 88, 89, 120	
6, 25, 44, 57, 141	72, 73, 74, 77, 129	
12, 13, 17, 35, 104	78, 79, 80, 81	
5, 19, 22, 30, 36, 37, 38, 40, 58, 59, 119, 130	82, 83, 84, 85, 91, 92, 93, 95, 96, 98	24, 47
52, 124		
8, 100		
39, 125	97, 126	

beside it is set to the final height; it has no tag and does not move.

All the steps that rise are set to a height equal to the floor. When they are activated, the steps will rise to the heights of 8, 16, 24, 32, . . . or 16, 32, 48, 64, ... The final nonmoving component of the staircase is set to its final height, so in a staircase composed of nine sectors that move with each rising 8, the final sector would have a height of 80 above the floor.

 **Lifts**

Lifts are simply sectors that travel between the heights of two other sectors. The lift must be built so that it

starts at the upper height. The lift will "remember" this height and return to it after it lowers.

If a lift sector is to be activated by a button or switch special, it must be constructed in the same manner as a door sector so that the line facings are correct for activation by pressing. For this reason, a lift sector should always be created by drawing it between two existing sectors; it should never be created first.

Creating a lift is very simple. A lift works and looks best if it has a slight buffer sector between it and the room it faces. Draw in the buffer sectors followed by the lift sector. Set the floor height of the lift to be equal to the floor height of the higher room. Tag the lift sector and assign a matching tag to the outside line on the upper room side. This line is assigned a line special type 88 or some similar type. This will cause the lift to be activated when the line is crossed.

A line special that is activated as a switch or button can be assigned to the side of the lift that is visible when the lift is in the upper position. This then allows a player to call the lift down by pressing the side of it in the same manner as a door. The special could also be used on a switch beside the door at the top or the bottom of the lift.

Examine LIFT.WAD on the enclosed disk for an example.

 Secrets

Secret areas in Doom are created through a combination of attributes and level planning. In some cases you may want to use the map itself to provide a hint that a secret area exists, by making it clear that there is a blank area on the map.

Secret Sector Attribute

The secret counter that is displayed at the end of each level reflects how many sectors with the "secret" attribute were located and entered by the player (Figure 5.23). The "secret" attribute must be assigned to sectors located in areas that you consider to be secret in order for this counter to accurately reflect what percentage of the secret areas were located by the player.

Secret Line Attribute

Lines also have a secret attribute, but it is not related to the secret counter. The secret attribute on a line causes the line to be displayed normally on the AutoMap. If this attribute is not used, a secret line that is designed to appear as a plain wall in Doom will display as a different color on the AutoMap and will thus no longer be a secret.

Secret Areas

The overall key to secret areas in Doom levels is this: What makes an area secret is that it is designed that

FIGURE 5.23

Players can see how many secret areas they have discovered.

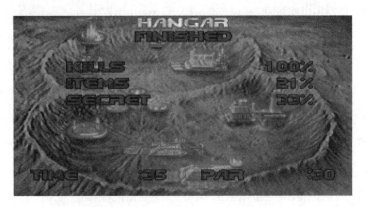

way in the level; use of attributes is secondary. In the original Doom levels, most secret areas are marked in some way. Typical markings include blinking lights and strange or misaligned textures. Some secret areas have doors triggered remotely so that you hear them or see them if you go into the area quickly enough. Others have windows that you can see through, but that leave you wondering how to get to the other side.

It is usually a good idea to follow a similar style in creating any secret areas in your levels. The player should never be reduced to pushing on every wall in the level trying to find the last secret level. There should be a logical way to locate all secrets, either by appearance or by careful inspection of the shape of the AutoMap.

Challenge but never frustrate the player. A frustrated player is not enjoying the level, and will eventually stop playing.

Continuing Your Level

Let's now continue constructing the level to the west in the space illustrated in Figure 5.24; this addition will be at a lower height. The main portion of this new area will be built inside a large sector, which will be attached to the original first room by a hallway with a lift in the middle.

Click on the first room to "pick up" its attributes, then draw the first portion of the connecting hall. This will allow this portion of the hall, which is higher, to match the floor and ceiling height of the room.

Next draw a fairly large sector like the one in Figure 5.25; this figure shows both the portion of this hall

FIGURE 5.24

Adding sectors to the west.

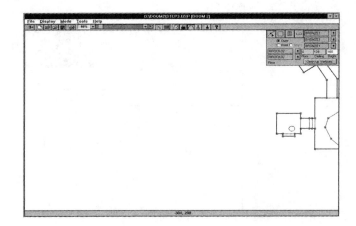

and the new large sector. Be sure that your new sector is far enough away from the other sectors so that there is room to fit the connecting hallway and lift.

Since the new area is to be below the first area, the height of its ceiling and floor should be dropped down. To lower a sector's height select it; then press PgDn repeatedly until you have reached the desired heights. Draw the western portion of the connecting hall, but be sure to leave space for the lift sector. In Figure 5.26, there is room enough for it to be square.

FIGURE 5.25

Adding a large sector.

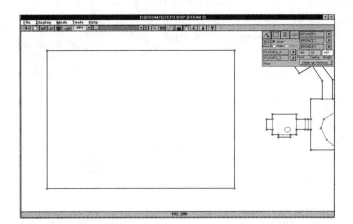

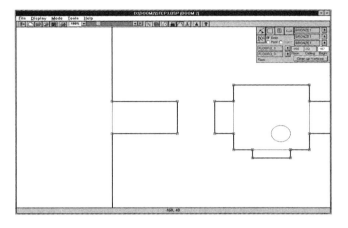

FIGURE 5.26

Add a hallway, leaving space for the lift.

Now draw in the lift sector. It should be at the same height as the upper adjacent sector, so select the upper adjacent sector first, then draw the lift sector as shown in Figure 5.27.

Now switch to Special/Texture mode by pressing P. You'll see the Line Special menu shown in Figure 5.28. You will need at least two line specials to make the lift work. On the upper side of the lift sector (coming from the east), the line special 88 is used—this will cause the lift to activate when the player walks onto the lift sector from that side. At the lower elevation side of the lift sector (coming from the west, or in this case, on the left side of the sector) a different line special, 62, is

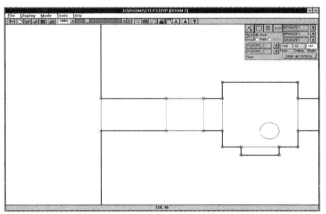

FIGURE 5.27

Add a lift at the height of the highest adjacent sector.

FIGURE 5.28

The Line Special

menu.

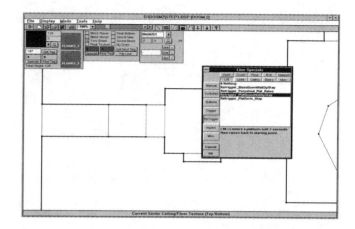

used on the lift sector side—this line special acts as a button (Figure 5.29). The button type of action is needed because the lift is normally in the upper position, and a player trying to enter from the west, that is, from the lower level, needs to be able to bring the lift to his or her height. This button type special lets the player "call" the lift by pressing its side. No equivalent method of activation is needed coming from the upper level (east), since the lift always returns to its upper position automatically.

Use a matching tag number for the lift sector and the two lines of the lift sector where you just assigned the line specials. Since this is the first special that we have

FIGURE 5.29

The lift button is placed in the lowest sector adjacent to the lift.

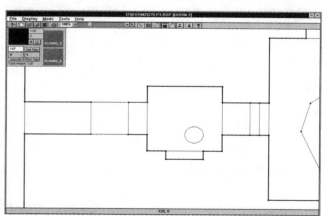

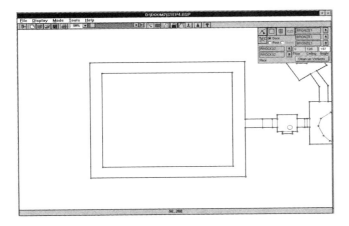

FIGURE 5.30

Transform a rectangular sector into a narrow corridor by adding a void in the middle.

used, the tags can all be set to 1. Jump into Doom and take a look at it. You should have a lift that works in both directions, and a very large open room.

If the lift doesn't work properly, make sure the sectors were drawn in the proper order and joined correctly. Next, check the line special values and make sure that both lines and the sector have matching tags.

Continuing with the level, let's transform the large sector that we drew into a large rectangular hallway by adding a void inside it (Figure 5.30). Don't forget to use the second mouse button when drawing out the void.

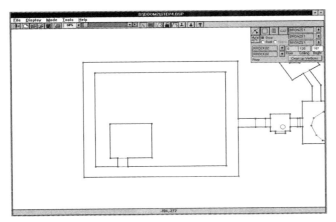

FIGURE 5.31

Add a small room inside the void.

FIGURE 5.32

Add a larger room

inside the void.

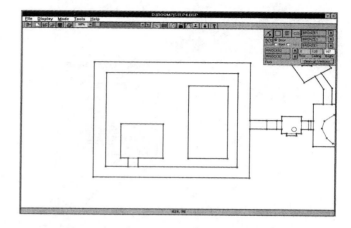

Now let's add two rooms to the area we've carved out by drawing the void. The rooms will be connected by a door, and in the second room we'll place the destination for the teleporter pad we created in Chapter 4.

First draw a small room inside the void, and use a short hallway to connect it to the outer hall (Figure 5.31). Then, to its right, draw a larger room inside the void (Figure 5.32). This is where the teleporter will go.

Next, connect the two rooms with a door (Figure 5.33). Use the AutoStruct tool to make it a red key door going east and west.

FIGURE 5.33

Add a door

between the

two rooms.

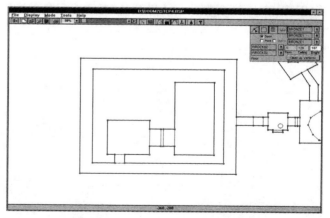

173

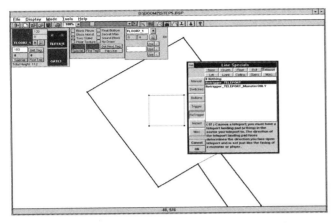

FIGURE 5.34

Adding line specials to make the teleporter work.

Next let's make the teleporter pad work. The pad, as you'll recall, is located in the skewed room to the northeast. The destination of the teleporter will be the larger of the two rooms we just drew (behind the red door) in the void of the western sector. Select each line of the teleporter pad in turn, and assign a teleporter special to it (Figure 5.34). The special used here is 97, ReTrigger_TELEPORT. This will allow the teleporter to be used repeatedly. The same tag number is assigned to all four lines, since the pad has the same destination from any side. The tag number that was assigned to the lines is now assigned to the destination sector.

Now, to indicate the destination for the teleporter, go to

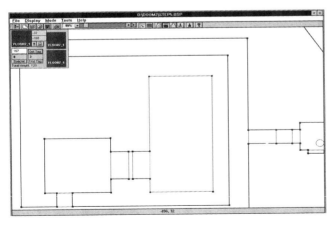

FIGURE 5.35

Picking the sector for the teleporter destination.

FIGURE 5.36

The teleporter destination object is selected.

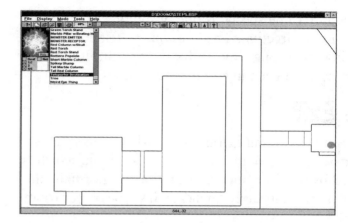

the destination sector and place a teleporter destination object into the sector (Figure 5.35 and 5.36). The placement and facing of this object are used to determine the location of players or monsters teleporting into the sector. The tag value of the sector matches the tag value of the line of the teleporter to indicate the target; the teleporter destination object is required to designate the exact placement of a player or monster that teleports (Figure 5.37).

Save the level and enter Doom. Use the teleporter pad. It doesn't work the way it should, does it? You can step onto the pad and nothing happens, but when you try to step *off* the pad you are teleported away. This is caused by the line facing.

FIGURE 5.37

The teleporter destination object has been inserted into the destination sector.

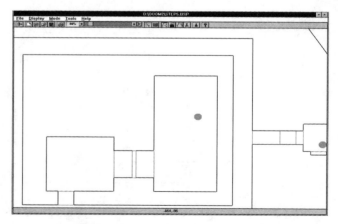

The teleporter line special is one of the types that only
works in one direction. The lines on the teleporter now
are facing the wrong way. To fix the operation of the
teleporter, select each line in turn and flip it.

The Exit

There is one more thing you should add to this level—
an exit switch. A Doom exit has a certain look, which is
achieved by the door and exit sign that are normally in
front of it. You can easily duplicate this type of exit room.

Start by drawing the exit room as shown in Figure 5.38.
(Don't forget to click on the area it will be connected to
first, so you can "pick up" the heights, brightness, and
textures.) Then add a door. If you are using the Auto-
Struct tool, pick north to south for this particular door
so that your level looks like Figure 5.39.

The exit sign should be placed near where the exit
switch will be (see Figure 5.40). The exit sign is a small
sector, 32 × 8, set inside the larger sector. Its ceiling is
16 below the larger sector.

The texture applied to the exit sign is (oddly enough)
called EXITSIGN (Figure 5.41). It is 64 wide and 16

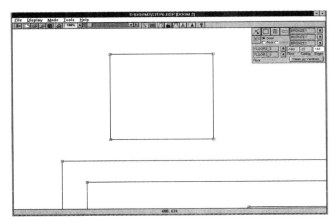

FIGURE 5.38

The exit room.

FIGURE 5.39

A door connecting the exit room to the western corridor.

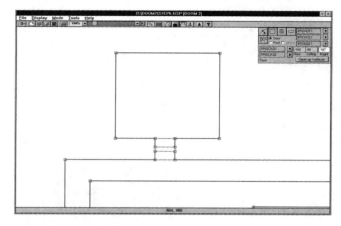

high, but only the left half is the EXIT portion of the sign. The rest of it is used for the side parts of the sign. Assign this texture to all four sides, but use a horizontal offset of 32 on the sides so that they show the gray portion of the texture and not the words. Check the height of the exit sign sector and make sure the floor is the same height as the surrounding room, and that the ceiling is 16 lower. You may also want to assign a different ceiling for this sector to give the sign more definition.

Assign the EXITDOOR texture to the sides of the door leading to this room (Figure 5.42). This lets the player recognize the exit easily. Notice that the EXITDOOR texture, like the EXITSIGN texture, is very wide, with

FIGURE 5.40

Place the exit sign in front of where you want the exit switch to go.

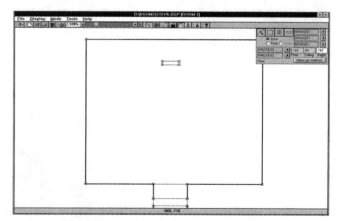

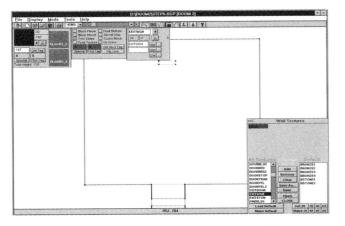

FIGURE 5.41

**Adding the
EXITSIGN texture
to the sign.**

two distinct texture maps. You can use these different
texture maps by using various horizontal offset values.

Now find a suitable texture to use for the exit switch
(Figure 5.43). This room was drawn in the BRONZE
family of textures, and SW1BRWN appears to be a fair
match. The texture is 128 × 128, so a wall section 128
wide must be prepared to take the wall texture.

Flip back to Structure mode, and then turn on the grid
so you can see how big a 128 line will be. Create two
breaks in the line along the back wall of the room
where the exit switch will be, and manipulate the points
until you have a line of the proper width (Figure 5.44).

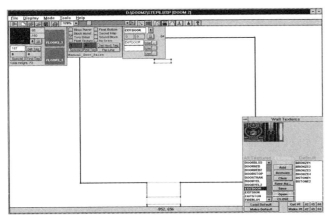

FIGURE 5.42

**Adding the EXIT-
DOOR texture to
the door leading
into the exit room.**

FIGURE 5.43

Selecting a texture

for the exit switch.

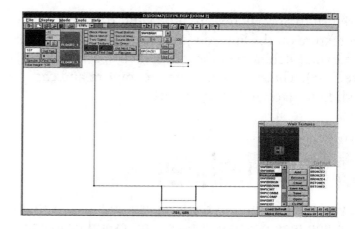

FIGURE 5.44

Creating a space

for the exit switch

along the back

wall.

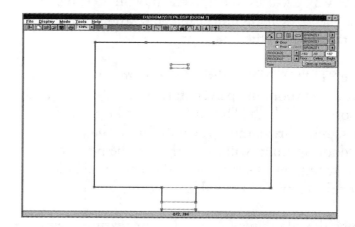

FIGURE 5.45

Assigning the exit

switch special to

the wall.

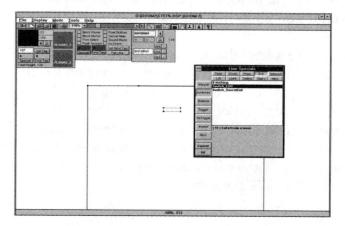

Now return to Special/Texture mode and paint the switch texture on the line you just created. To make it into an exit switch, assign the exit switch special, 11 (Figure 5.45). The exit room is now complete and can be used. Enter Doom and try it out!

Fixing Textures

When you walk around in the level as you have created it so far, you may notice that there are several problems with the way textures line up. The most noticeable of these is the vertical alignment of the textures, especially above the doors in the first room.

The file STEP8.WAD on disk shows many fixes for the textures. The room the player starts in is 128 high, and the doors are 72 high. This difference in height is 56, and assigning this as the vertical offset on the textures at the door openings will cause them to be perfectly aligned with the walls to either side. The same holds true for the textures in the alcove sectors.

Examine this file to make sure all your textures align properly with the walls. Pay particular attention to the wall section containing the exit switch.

You now have a level that contains a teleporter, a lift, and an exit. You are well on your way to creating fully functional Doom levels. Continue working with this level on your own and build upon it and the skills you have learned. If you make a mistake, remember that you can always go back to one of the automatic back-up files created by the editor. See Appendix B for details on editor file management.

Designing Levels for DeathMatch

The most popular type of new level is the DeathMatch level. It is the multiplayer feature of Doom that has unquestionably led to its great popularity and longevity. This chapter will help you focus on those elements of level design that contribute to great DeathMatch levels.

 # What Makes a Good DeathMatch Level?

Most levels that are fun for a single player are worthless for DeathMatch play, and vice versa. A single player is out to beat the odds, cutting through hordes of demons and avoiding devious tricks and traps. A DeathMatch player just wants to find his or her friends fast and make their day. Creating good DeathMatch levels is an art form. Here are a few guidelines for creating quality DeathMatch levels:

- *Keep it simple.* A good DeathMatch level should generally have 80–120 sectors. When levels are much larger than that, it simply takes players too long to find each other.
- *Avoid extraneous objects.* The larger the number of objects, the more information that has to be dealt with over the connection. This can slow down game play. If it isn't needed, don't put it in.
- *Use lots of barrels.* Sounds of explosions are fun clues to where action is going on. Interesting strategy can be developed around barrels, and they do not respawn.

- *Have few or no monsters.* You are there to fight each other, not the computer. Especially avoid using close-quarter monsters like the Demon, and

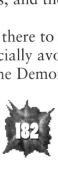

never use Lost Souls or Pain Elementals. Only use Cacodemons in large open spaces where people can run away if they choose.

- *Consider the weapon stock carefully.* This will depend on the style of DeathMatch play you enjoy. Many people believe the weapon stocking should be mainly Shotguns and Chainguns. If there is a larger weapon like a Plasma or Rocket Launcher, it should be an object that is tough to get to but easy to guard. It should always be difficult to get powerful weapons and ammo.

- *Don't forget to use texture and lighting.* Use a variety of texture and lighting effects to keep the level interesting. Dark murky areas are effective for hiding, while opponents who suddenly find themselves in a well-lit room will be easy targets. Yes, you can be an interior decorator *and* a bloodthirsty fiend.

- *Avoid creating "pill box" situations.* A player should never be able to hide and regain weapons or health at the same time. Always put weapons, ammo, and health in open or hard-to-reach areas.

- *Don't forget the exit.* You may want to use a "cooperative" exit where two or more players must act together to activate the exit switch (suggestions for how to do this are given later in this chapter).

Thin walkways over lava or nuke pits are also entertaining—especially if you have to cross them to get to something good. Try to be creative; follow the guidelines but don't be rigid about it. And if you don't agree with one of the guidelines, to heck with it.

Respawn vs. None

Games using version 1.4 or higher of the Doom engine have the option of using DeathMatch 2 rules. Death-Match play with these rules is superior because items such as weapons, ammo, and health will respawn.

Players are penalized for causing their own death. This allows for more balanced play and improves the strategies involved.

DeathMatch levels should generally be designed specifically for either DM2 rules or the original rules. Levels designed for use before DM2 tend to have far too much ammo and too many weapons lying about to make DM2 play fun. Make sure you indicate to people who might use your level which set of rules you designed your level for. Almost everyone prefers the DM2 rules, so you can generally be fine designing only for DM2.

Ledges

One of the most popular DeathMatch levels to date is LEDGES.WAD by Mark Gresbach. The level has been followed up by LEDGES II, III, and IV, as well as revisions for DM2 rules. The same author has also designed several levels specifically for Doom Tournament play.

Ledges has remained a consistently popular DeathMatch level because it is small; the revised level LEDGESI for DM2 rules is a masterpiece in short and brutal DeathMatch play (Figure 6.1).

The level has lots of DeathMatch start locations—no less than 12 start locations on a map of only 109 sectors. This is great, because there is nothing worse than reappearing and being blown away before you even have a chance to get your bearings.

There are few Monsters—just a few lonesome Cacodemons in the central "pit" to make people run for cover at the start, and all in the open.

The most common weapon on the level is a Shotgun, but there is a Chaingun, a Chain Saw, and a Rocket Launcher on exposed ledges, and a Plasma Gun and BFG that daring folks can make a try for. Trying to get the Plasma Gun is usually a good way to get yourself killed if there are more than two players.

The pit design keeps players from being able to completely stop each other from gaining access to any other part of the map. If you get trapped by another player, you just jump into the pit and run for it. There are no dead ends and no place from which you can cover every point of access to your own location or the location of a key item. At the same time, there is enough cover that a player who keeps on the move can stay away from someone who has gained weapons superiority.

There is abundant health and armor, but in small doses. This forces players to keep on the move to regain their points while preventing hoarding.

The central feature of Ledges is the elevator (see Figure 6.2). It is as simple as it is effective. You must use the

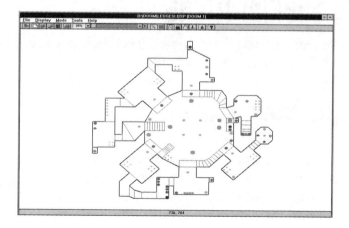

FIGURE 6.1

The Ledges DeathMatch level.

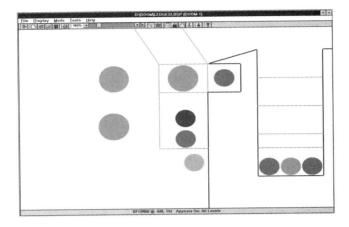

FIGURE 6.2

The best weapons are reached through this exposed elevator.

elevator in order to reach the Plasma Gun or the BFG. The only catch is that you must wait for it a long time—long enough for someone to realize what you are up to. To make things worse, the room with the BFG in it is placed in such a way that you must jump off the elevator, then wait for it again in order to get out; meanwhile, anyone who has noticed you has time to get in position to nail you.

Special Tricks

After you master basic DeathMatch level design, spice up your levels with these techniques.

Cooperative Exits

One annoying thing that can occur during a Death-Match game is someone exiting the level before everyone else is ready to continue. Sometimes the player exits deliberately, but other times a "Doom reflex" takes over and the player hits a button by instinct.

To prevent this from happening, you can create cooperative exits. The most common way to design a cooperative exit is to block the exit switch with a door that is opened by a button at some distance away—far enough away that it is impossible to run from the button to the door in time to get through. One player will have to trip the door button in order for another player to reach the exit switch. This can be repeated to create exits that require the cooperation of three or even four players.

Tag Team

Two-on-two-player games can be lots of fun. Take advantage of the new possibilities when designing a level for this kind of play. Areas of the level can be blocked with doors that can only be opened by two players working together. These could include entire sections of the map, or perhaps a closet with the Plasma inside it.

Puzzles can be created that require two players working together to get through. You can create doors that can only be opened from one side; a player who enters without support becomes trapped. You can even liven up the action by putting a switch in that activates a crushing ceiling.

Warning Flash

This technique can allow other players to be warned when someone enters a particular area of the map. Setting up a combination of line specials 17 and 35 (or others as you see fit), you can create triggers that activate as someone enters an area and deactivate as the player leaves. These triggers can then be linked to remote sectors that will flash to warn the other players.

DeathMatch Caveats

When you create your DeathMatch masterpiece, remember to make it please you. It should match the particular style of play that you and your friends enjoy.

You might want to provide your friends with maps of DeathMatch levels you create. Otherwise you may be creating an unfair advantage—or at least the appearance of one—when playing those levels.

Have fun, and remember: Those who run away live to fight another day!

Advanced Design

 Zen and the Art of Doom Level Design

A wise student of Doom level design will pay attention to all the details. By learning how the specific dimensions of your level (room layout, monster and weapon placement, etc.) affect game play, you will be able to create levels that are more fun to play.

Doom Geometry

Doom space, both vertical and horizontal, is measured in a unit that is equivalent to one pixel on screen. For instance, the actual bitmap graphic for a floor tile is 64 × 64 pixels, and on the map the floor tile takes up an area that measures 64 × 64 units. The player graphic is 56 pixels high, and in the game, the player is 56 units high (or tall).

This system of measurement makes it very simple to calculate texture sizes, offsets, and placements.

Being aware of the sizes of objects and the structures around them is important for reasons mentioned earlier in this book. To help you work with measurements, the editor displays the width of every object you are working with. It is also helpful to remember that most monsters are the same height, 56 units—the exceptions are the Hell Baron (64), Cyberdemon (110), and the Spider Demon (100).

The clearance between the floor and ceiling of a sector must be at least equal to the height of the monster or player in order for them to be able to pass through. The interface between sectors must also be adequately high for passage between them.

In order for an object (such as a player) to pass through a hallway or opening, the opening must be *wider* than the object. A player's width is 32; an opening of 33 (only 1 unit greater) will permit a player to pass through, but can only be entered with care.

Theoretically, monsters can pass through openings nearly as narrow as they are, but they usually won't. The logic monsters follow in moving is simple: They go after the players whenever possible, they don't walk off a drop more than 24 units high, and they don't like confined spaces.

If you want monsters to travel, make the spaces as wide and level as possible (meaning no drastic changes in floor levels). The run of a stair in relation to its rise is important if you want monsters to travel up stairs—make your stairs long with a gentle rise. Of course, flying creatures don't care about stairs.

TABLE 7.1 Minimum Hall Width and Stair Run for Monsters to Pass		
Type	**Hall Width**	**Step Run**
Former Humans	44	34
Imp	44	34
Demon/Spectre	64	51
Cacodemon	64	n/a
Lost Soul	64	n/a
Hell Baron	64	41

Table 7.1 details the minimum hall width and stair run for a monster to pass. The stair run assumes a rise of 24. These are the minimum passage widths; for easy passage, a larger opening is better. Naturally, if the monster is hot on your heels, it will go through the minimum hall width easily.

Level Limits

The coordinates used for the map are limited to the range of an integer variable, or between −32768 and 32767. These coordinates represent the outer limits for any level; a single level will not necessarily use the full available range, but no single coordinate can be less than −32768 or greater than 32767. The maximum size a level can be is limited by the blockmap, which cannot contain more than about 13,000 entries. Each block in the blockmap is 128 units square, so the largest square level that could be created is approximately 14,400 units high and wide [(square root of 13,000) * 128].

A level designed to be as wide as possible would be 512 blocks wide (65,536/128) and 25 blocks high, or approximately 65,000 × 3,200 units. It's very unlikely that you will ever approach these limits, but now you know how to calculate if your level fits within the limits of the Doom engine.

Real-Life Measurements

If you are creating a map based on an actual place, it might be helpful to use the following numbers. For horizontal measurements, 16 map units can be considered approximately equal to 1 foot (48 units equal 1 meter). For vertical measurements, 1 unit can be considered approximately equal to 1 inch (a vertical mea-

surement of 12 units actually comes out to be slightly less that 1 foot, but using 12 vertical units to equal 1 foot will look about right).

I use these equivalences because they make computations easy; however, if you've been doing the math, you probably have realized that the numbers result in a very short player—about $4\frac{1}{2}$ feet tall.

Doom Physics

Doom has its own physics system. It is a bit cartoonish in that the player can fall any distance without harm, but fairly realistic in most other respects.

EXPLOSIONS

Barrel explosions have a radius of 128 units. The force of a blast can shift the position of other barrels or ignite them. For a chain-effect explosion, keep barrels within 64 units of each other—outside of that radius they cannot be guaranteed to explode.

JUMPING

The player can "jump" across openings by simply running right across them. The widest opening that can be crossed between two platforms at the same height is 136 units. At distances of more than 136, the destination platform has to be lower than the starting platform; at distances less than 136 it can actually be higher.

Table 7.2 shows the maximum horizontal distance that can be crossed for each difference in height, measured from the starting platform to the destination. A negative

TABLE 7.2	Differences in Platform Heights in Relation to Distances Players Can Jump
Height	**Horizontal Distance of Jump**
−46	224
−20	184
0	136
16	88
24	48

number in the Height column indicates that the destination platform is lower than the starting platform, while a positive number indicates that it is higher.

Advanced Structure Manipulation

This section describes more complex effects that you can create through the careful manipulation of the sectors on your Doom levels.

Bisected Sectors

In some cases you may want to have a line running through a sector without creating two separate sectors. In this case the line that runs through the middle has the same sector on both sides. This trick is typically used for blocking sounds (so that a sound made on one side of the line is not heard on the other), or for triggering a special event.

FIGURE 7.1

Two sectors ready to be split.

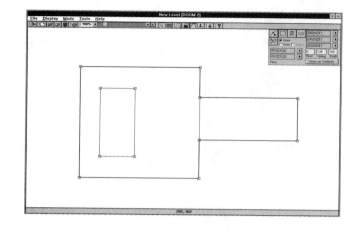

You can use the following procedure for dividing a sector in two with a line. This procedure works for an inside sector as well as for a stand-alone sector. The accompanying figures demonstrate how to add a line to both types of sectors.

Figure 7.1 shows a few sectors. We will make two splits: one through the inner sector on the left, and another through the hall on the right. In each case, the sector will remain a single sector.

Insert three vertexes on one side of the sector where you want the split, and add a single vertex on the other

FIGURE 7.2

Adding vertexes where you want the splits to occur.

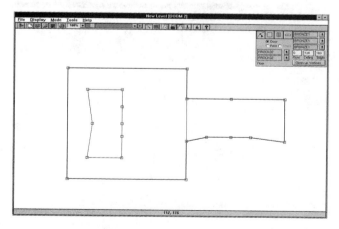

195

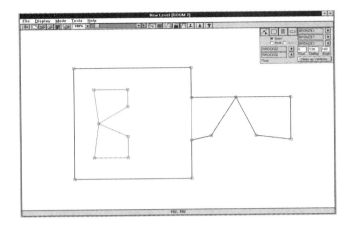

FIGURE 7.3

Dragging the
middle vertex
to the vertex on
the other side of
the sector.

side of the sector (Figure 7.2). Then drag the middle
vertex and join it with the single vertex on the other
side of the sector (Figure 7.3).

For each of the sectors, there are two new vertexes that
you haven't moved yet—the vertexes that surrounded
the middle vertex. Drag these two vertexes together so
that you get something that looks like Figure 7.4. Now
your new lines are formed, but without creating new
sectors. You can move the lines or change their angle
by dragging either of their vertexes.

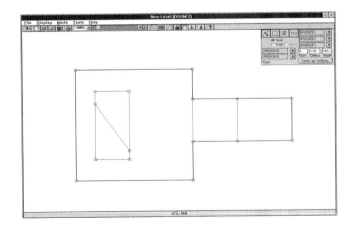

FIGURE 7.4

Drag the two
remaining vertexes
together.

Advanced Lighting

You must learn to follow the path of light. Scrupulous attention should be paid to the use of lighting at all times—even the experts make mistakes in this area.

Look closely at the entryway to MAP01 from Doom II (Figure 7.5). It looks very cool—the triangular steps come toward you, with varying brightness. But where is the light coming from? It seems to be coming from the bright hallway. Then what makes the light shaped in the strange triangles that follow the steps below?

The answer is, nothing. There is no good reason for the light to be shaped that way on the ceiling, and it looks strange. Simply noticing that type of thing will lead to much better looking levels.

The effect of the changing brightness on the steps in this entryway is very good and appropriate; it is only the ceiling that looks odd. The simplest solution to this particular lighting problem is to raise the roof. If the ceiling is raised high enough that it can't be seen, the effect is of

FIGURE 7.5

Cool lighting effects in the original entryway to MAP01 of Doom II.

FIGURE 7.6

*Revised lighting
scheme for MAP01.*

a cathedral ceiling with an unseen light source above (a skylight?). The wall texture is complex enough and vertically aligned so that you don't notice striping on it the way it was noticeable on the ceiling, so that is fine as is. In fact, it looks quite good, with light apparently reflecting off the wall from above (Figure 7.6).

This lighting problem was fixed not by changing the lighting, but by a simple structural change.

The demonstration file KOOL.WAD, which is on the disk with this book, has several examples of truly

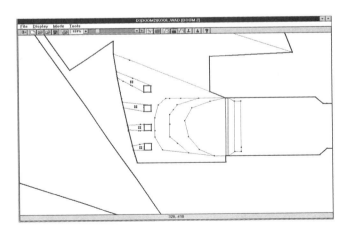

FIGURE 7.7

*This area of
KOOL.WAD
demonstrates
advanced lighting
techniques.*

FIGURE 7.8

The columns appear to cast shadows on the wall, ceiling, and floor.

advanced lighting. The first of these is in the area of four columns, found to the east of the large KOOL on the map (Figure 7.7). These columns appear to cast shadows on the wall, ceiling, and floor (Figure 7.8).

There are several techniques used here to achieve something never seen in the original levels of Doom. Notice the shadows. It appears that light streaming in the partially open door is causing shadows of the four

FIGURE 7.9

A glow of light seems to come from under the door.

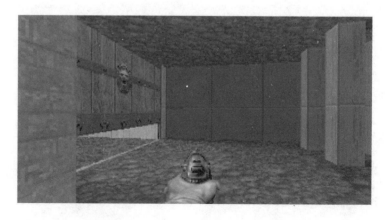

columns to be cast onto the wall, ceiling, and floor (Figure 7.8). This is a fairly simple effect to achieve.

Now look closely at the floor in front of the door (Figure 7.9). There is a "glow" across the floor that fades with distance from the door. The effect looks very much like light being cast from a diffuse light source behind the door. Walk around and look at it closely. Doesn't it look great?

After a player opens the door and walks through it, specials are triggered that cause the light level of the room to increase as it should if the door is open and there is a brighter room beyond. For instance, the brightness of the shadows is raised (Figure 7.10). Once the door is open all the way, the brightness of the room is increased to its maximum level (Figure 7.11).

To watch this lighting effect occur, open the door, then exit the room at a normal pace. Turn around and come back into the room and you will see the change in brightness. This technique is not perfect. The triggers depend on the player passing through the door. If the door is opened without going through, the brightness level does not change appropriately.

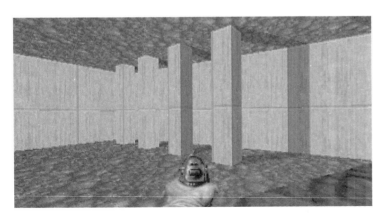

FIGURE 7.10

The shadows become lighter when the brightness of the room increases.

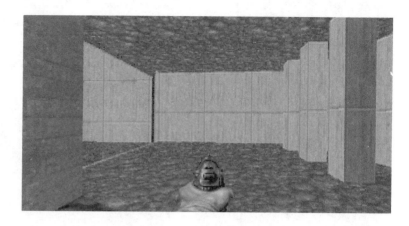

FIGURE 7.11

The room is brighter after the door opens.

Getting the shadows to increase in brightness by an appropriate amount is the most complex thing about this demonstration. The brightness level that the shadow sectors will change to has to be tightly controlled to look right. The method used here is to create a very small sector containing the brightness level that will be changed to and then to use a special that will cause the brightness of the shadow sectors to rise to the level of that adjacent sector. This sector is hidden within the shadow sectors as a contained sector and is considered adjacent for the purpose of line special actions. The small sector is hidden by raising the floor and lowering the ceiling of the sector enough that they are not drawn on the screen.

Textures for the sides are also omitted, causing nothing to be drawn for this small sector. In order to understand how this works on the screen, consider how the Doom engine works. The Doom engine starts at the point furthest from the player and draws in flat and wall textures until it reaches the view point of the player. By making the floor of this contained sector much higher and the ceiling much lower compared to the surrounding sector, and by not specifying any texture for the walls, the Doom engine never draws the sector on

screen. This is a limitation of the Doom engine that we are exploiting, and an abnormal level structure that is created to deliberately get this effect.

Making Good Use of Difficulty Levels

Don't neglect difficulty levels. Not everyone has the reflexes or killer instinct to blaze through at the highest difficulty levels. The difficulty settings were put there for a reason.

Use more monsters or nastier monsters at higher difficulty settings, and more first aid and better weapons at lower settings. When placing objects, you may find it easiest to start out by stocking for the medium difficulty setting. You can then go back later and add or change monsters appropriately.

Table 7.3 shows how many times a player must shoot a monster with a particular weapon in order to kill it. A monster's toughness obviously affects the difficulty of a level.

A useful technique when stocking for difficulty levels is to have different types of monsters at different difficulty settings. Use a trooper in place of a sergeant at the lowest difficulty level, a Cacodemon in place of a pain elemental, and so on. You can place the two monsters in the same place on the map, but have only one of them present at a given difficulty level. However, if you use the stocking strategy of an easy monster at the low

TABLE 7.3	How Many Hits It Takes to Kill a Monster				
Creature	**Pistol**	**Shotgun**	**Rocket**	**Plasma**	**BFG**
Trooper	2	1	1	1	1
Sergeant	3	1	1	2	1
SS Trooper	5	1	1	3	1
Imp	6	1	1	3	1
CG Dude	7	1	1	4	1
Lost Soul	10	2	1	5	1
Player	10	2	2	5	1
Demon	14	2	1	7	1
Spectre	14	2	1	7	1
Revenant	30	5	2	15	1
Cacodemon	36	6	2	18	1
Pain Elemental	40	6	2	20	1
Arachnotron	50	8	3	25	1
Hell Knight	50	8	3	25	1
Mancubus	60	9	3	30	1
Archvile	70	10	4	35	1
Hell Baron	100	15	5	50	1
Spiderdemon	300	43	15	150	2
Cyberdemon	400	58	20	200	3

est level, a harder monster at the middle level, and both at the highest difficulty level, be sure *not* to place monsters on top of each other, so they will be free to move when they are both present.

Items

Place more ammo and better guns at lower difficulty settings. As a general rule, at the highest difficulty setting there should be slightly less than enough ammo to kill everything on the level; at the medium difficulty setting there should be slightly more equipment than needed to complete the level, and at the easiest difficulty setting there should be nearly twice as much as needed.

There should be more health available at the easier settings. Place medkits on the easiest settings, stimpacks on the medium settings, and potions or nothing at the most difficult settings.

At easier settings you may want to be more forgiving with radiation suits and light amp goggles as well.

Traps

You can spare players from particularly nasty traps at lower difficulty settings by using obstacles. Block access to a trip line or opening. Lamp and Column items work well for this purpose. If you do block off areas at different difficulties, don't mark any of the blocked sectors as secret, or you will drive the player nuts looking for them.

Special Tricks for Climbing Walls

It is possible to create "walls" that the player can "climb." The secret to this technique is that it is possible to make steps that are as thin as a single unit yet that the player can still walk across. A set of such thin stairs will look like a wall, but can be ascended and descended like a normal staircase. By adjusting the lower texture vertical offsets or using a texture that aligns easily and also using a floor texture that blends in, you can create what appears to be a wall. The player can fly right up—a wall as high as 192 units can be scaled in the space of 8 horizontal units.

The only problem with this sort of unusual structure is that players aren't aware it can exist. If you use this in a WAD that is intended for single-player action, make sure that either it is not vital the player realize the structure is there, or the player has no choice but to hit it.

Rock climbing can be very entertaining in DeathMatch levels, and can be used to create new strategies. Obviously, the physical structure causes monsters to ignore it.

To build the structure, create a normal staircase first, with steps 16 or so units wide. Once the stairs are created, turn off the Snap-to grid and carefully move the vertexes in closer to the wall until the spacing is only one unit wide for each step.

 # Changing DOOM.EXE

The ultimate level of Doom editing is actually changing the behavior of the game. Thanks to a lot of work on the part of many people, the Doom executable is understood well enough that it is possible to make changes to it.

Included on the CD is the program DEHACKED, created by Greg Lewis. This program makes performing modifications fairly easy.

CHAPTER 7

Before you do anything in this section, make a backup copy of DOOM.EXE and DOOM2.EXE.

The changes you make with the executable editor will make changes to the behavior of Doom. This will affect Doom at all times, including when you are playing the original levels. If you play DeathMatch with a modified Doom, make sure all players have their executable modified in precisely the same way or it will crash.

Setting Up DEHACKED

Unzip the archive into your DOOM or DOOM2 directory.

First you need to get your DEHACKED.INI file in order. Edit this file and put your full path and name to your Doom executable and Master WAD files. Then change the Doom Version according to the version of Doom you are editing, as follows: If you are using an old version of Doom (version 1.2), set this equal to 0. If you are using Doom 1.666 or Doom II *higher* than 1.666, set it equal to 1. If you are using Doom II version 1.666, set it equal to 2. Note that if you have Doom II version 1.7a, this version of DEHACKED will complain that it isn't sure what version of Doom you are using. Press Y to continue.

The Main Screen

When the executable editor first starts, it displays the attributes of the Player object type (Figure 7.12). The top left box shows information about the current object. Scroll through the different object types with the PgUp and PgDn keys.

206

DEHACKED's

main screen.

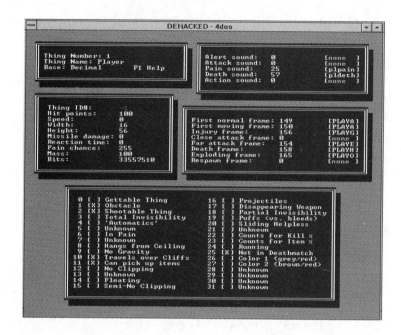

You will notice that there are objects for everything that you ever see in the game—different monsters, fireballs, teleporter pad flashes, and so on. The behavior and appearance of the object types are differentiated by their graphics, sounds, values, and bit settings.

Objects with a Thing ID# of −1 cannot be placed directly into level THINGS data. Fireballs are spawned by creatures that shoot them, rockets and other projectiles are spawned when you fire, and players are spawned by the player start positions.

By studying the settings each type of object has by default and carefully manipulating these settings, you can create new monsters, weapons, and effects.

The way the Doom engine is structured makes this type of editing quite easy. For example, when you set the name of the graphic to be used for an object, the

engine will automatically look at what graphics match that pattern and follow the animation correctly without your needing to set it by hand.

Basic Usage

Let's see how DEHACKED works by making a simple change in appearance. Hit PgDn once so you are on the TROOPER object type. Hit the right arrow twice; the number for "First normal frame" will highlight. Press the down arrow six times so that "Exploding frame" is highlighted. This number is set to 165 right now. This is the number of the frame that starts the graphic sequence of the trooper being blown into a pile of giblets. Press Enter and you will be prompted for a new value. If you are using Doom II, enter 281; if you are using Doom, enter 127. The graphic name will change to either FIREA or MISLB.

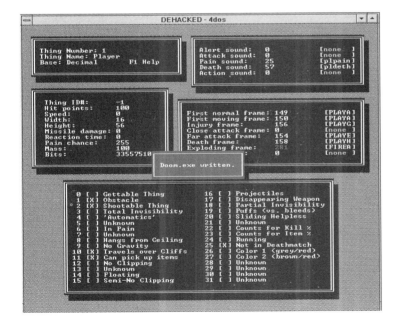

FIGURE 7.13

Saving your changes to DOOM.EXE.

Press W to write the changes to the Doom executable (Figure 7.13). Then press Exit and run Doom. To quickly see the effect of what you just did, use the cheat keys IDFA to get ammo and switch to the rocket launcher. Now find a trooper and nail him at close range. Boom! The trooper will burst into flames or explode and disappear, depending on your version of Doom.

Continuing with DEHACKED

Documentation for DEHACKED and a list of creative things to do with it are on the CD with the program. DEHACKED.TXT contains an introduction and credits from the author of the program, README.TXT contains instructions for setting up and using the program, and DHEFUN02.TXT contains instructions for fun things to do with the program.

Please note that you cannot redistribute modified Doom executables to friends or through means such as uploading to a BBS. The documentation contains instructions on creating a patch file (DEH), which is a list of instructions DEHACKED can follow to duplicate the changes that have been made to another copy of Doom. If you wish to share your modifications you must follow this procedure of creating a DEH file.

Have Fun and Be Creative

Use the techniques and skills you have learned from this book as the basis for your art. The CD accompanying this book contains many hundreds of user-created levels. Some of these are quite excellent and should be studied and emulated. Don't be locked into a

pattern of design and thought by the levels you have played and seen; be creative and don't be afraid to experiment. Many exciting and unique techniques have already been discovered or created using the Doom engine, and you may find even more.

Doom is already being followed by many other games of its type, and many more are sure to follow. A new tradition of user-created levels has been born; the process of three-dimensional thinking and design that you use in creating Doom levels will be equally applicable to future games and Virtual Reality applications.

What's on the
CD-ROM and
How to Install It

The disk contains a valuable collection of software, including the Renegade Graphics Doom Editor, sound and music editors, and many other utilities that will help you build and check your Doom levels. You will also find hundreds of WAD files to play and learn from.

How to Install the Files on Disk

To install the editor, start Windows and select File/Run from the Program Manager. Run the SETUP program in the RENEGADE directory on the CD. Read the README.TXT file, which is displayed after you complete the installation, and follow any further instructions it contains. The other .ZIP files can simply be extracted into your Doom or Doom2 directory. Each one contains documentation in the form of a .TXT or .DOC file. The .WAD files can be placed directly into your Doom or Doom2 directory.

Look for the file CDGUIDE in the main directory of the CD for a more complete guide to the contents. The main directories of interest on the CD are:

RENEGADE The installation files for the level editor

BOOK Files and levels specifically mentioned in the book

SOUND New sounds and music

SOUND/UTIL Sound and Music utilities

GRAPHICS New graphics

GAPHICS/UTIL Graphics utilities

LEVELS New Doom and Doom II levels

DEATHMATCH Doom and Doom II DeathMatch levels

UTIL Doom-related utilities

 # Getting Updates

The latest possible versions of the software for this book have been included on the disk. Much of this software is being updated constantly, so you may eventually want to look for more recent versions. If you register any of the software, you will of course receive the latest version.

Many megabytes of utilities, sounds, graphics, and WAD files are available online. Some of the places you might try are Internet sites and BBSs.

The latest version of the editor used in this book is always available on the Renegade Graphics BBS (home of the author).

Internet

The best Internet sites for Doom are constantly changing. In general it is best to read the Doom-specific newsgroups for the latest information on Doom-related files on the Net. There is also a Doom binaries newsgroup.

The following FTP sites have been good sources of Doom-related material; however, we cannot guarantee that they will continue to carry such material:

ftp.orst.edu   /pub/gaming/DOOM/

empires.stanford.edu /pub/

ftp.uni-erlangen.de
/pub/pc/msdos/games/ID/DOOM-stuff/

ftp.uwp.edu   /pub/msdos/games/id/home-brew/Doom/

infant2.sphs.indiana.edu

wuarchive.wustl.edu
/pub/MSDOS_UPLOADS/games/Doomstuff/

If you have mail-only access to the Internet, you can send e-mail to:

```
mail-server@mimosa.astro.indiana.edu
```

In the text of the mail, put the lines:

```
send help
end
```

You will be mailed instructions on using the e-mail ftp service.

BBSs

There are many BBSs that are mostly or entirely dedicated to Doom. Some of these include:

Renegade Graphics BBS 615-337-9198

Lithium BBS   510-455-0425

Doom Support BBS   510-494-0675 (not associated with id Software)

WC BBS   510-937-0156

Software Creations   508-368-7036

Exec-PC   414-789-4500

MetroDoom BBS 404-590-9375

Game Palace   305-587-4258

These BBSs also offer four-player Doom via modem:

H2H Online   619-426-0073

APCi   618-632-7664

 # Shareware

Many of the programs included on the disk are shareware. You are encouraged to register them. The following information from the Association of Shareware Professionals may help you to understand more about shareware.

What Is "Shareware"?

"Shareware" is a term that describes a unique marketing approach for software. Shareware, unlike its commercial counterparts, may be freely copied and passed around. It may be distributed by electronic bulletin boards (BBSs), computer clubs, and disk libraries. The authors of the programs, however, retain all legal rights to the software (a copyright). They also request or require that people who try their software and decide to use it send a "registration fee" (which is equivalent to purchasing the software).

Isn't It "Public Domain"?

No! Public domain software has been released completely to the public, and the author retains no legal

rights. Shareware authors, on the other hand, hold copyright on their programs. Just as for commercial software, the shareware programmer's software is protected by U.S. and international copyright law.

What Do I Get If I Register?

Many shareware companies offer printed documentation, disks, and telephone support as incentives for users to register their shareware. Some companies also offer free updates and commissions. But the most important benefit of registration is that you receive a legal license to continue using the software.

Aren't Registration Payments Voluntary?

No. While some authors indicate that payment is voluntary, their willingness to give their software away does not modify the rights of other authors. If a shareware program's documentation clearly states that a registration payment is required for regular use, then you are bound by law to register or stop using the program.

Does This Idea Actually Work?

Yes. But it depends on you, the user. If you as a user find a program you like, it is imperative that you register it. Only through receiving registrations can shareware authors receive the monetary and, more importantly, moral support to keep working on new and better software.

Doom Editor
Reference

 The Keyboard

The keyboard controls of the Doom Editor do not always follow typical Windows program usage. For example, the Del key is never used for deleting. The keyboard commands are shown in Table B.1.

Although some of the key commands may seem odd to you at first, users find that it does not take long to learn them, and to make very efficient use of the editor.

TABLE B.1	DOOM Editor Keyboard Controls
Key	**Effect**
T	Go to Thing (Object) mode and/or set to object Move/Inspect mode
I	Go to Thing mode and/or set to Object Insert/Delete mode
V	Vertex mode. Go to Structure mode or switch to Vertex tool
P	Go to Special/Line(paint) mode
L or S	Go to Structure mode with the Sector tool active, or switch to the Sector tool if already in Structure mode
Spacebar	Refresh map display
Ctrl+S	Quicksave to QUIKSAVE.BSP in editor directory
G	Toggle display of map grid
Shift+G	Change size of grid snap
Ctrl+Y	Toggle Snap-to grid

TABLE B.1 Continued

Key	Effect
+ −	Zoom the map display in and out (holding Shift or Alt makes Zoom work in larger increments)
Arrows	Pan map display 1/4 screen in selected direction
C	Center map on next selected point
Shift+C	Center map and zoom on next selected point

THING/OBJECT MODE

I	Set Insert/Delete object mode
T	Set Move/Inspect object mode
Ctrl+O	Toggle on-screen object labels

SPECIAL/TEXTURE MODE

The floor/ceiling heights and brightness of the currently selected sector can be changed with keyboard controls for speed. All of these normally increment by 8, but holding Shift causes the increment to be 1, and Alt causes it to be 32.

[and]	Decrease/increase sector brightness
Ins Del	Raise/lower floor height
Home End	Raise/lower ceiling height
PgUp PgDn	Raise/lower floor *and* ceiling height, moving entire room up or down
Ctrl+1, 2, 3, 4	Switch to the corresponding palette (see "Managing Palettes" later in this appendix)

(Continues)

TABLE B.1 Continued

Key	Effect

STRUCTURE MODE

The same controls used to modify the current sector in Special/Texture mode can be used to modify the settings of the next sector to be drawn.

Key	Effect
D	Delete the currently selected sector

With a sector selected (highlighted green):

Key	Effect
[and]	Decrease/increase sector brightness
Ins and Del	Raise/lower floor height
Home and End	Raise/lower ceiling height
PgUp and PgDn	Raise/lower floor *and* ceiling height, moving entire room up or down

With no sector selected, these affect the next sector to be drawn:

Key	Effect
[and]	Decrease/increase brightness of next sector to be drawn
Ins and Del	Raise/lower floor height of next sector to be drawn
Home and End	Raise/lower ceiling height of next sector to be drawn
PgUp and PgDn	Raise/lower floor and ceiling height, moving entire room up or down for next sector to be drawn

You will probably be most efficient in editing by using the arrow keys to pan around the display and the + and − to zoom in and out. Be aware that holding the Alt key while zooming in and out increases the amount of change in zoom level; the Shift key also increases the amount of zoom, but by a lesser amount.

The Screen

The toolbar controls from left to right are listed in Table B.2.

TABLE B.2	DOOM Editor Toolbar Controls
Command	**Effect**
Exit	Quit the editor
New	Start working with a blank map
Open Level	Get one of the original Doom levels
Open WAD	Open a .BSP or .WAD file
Save	Save the current work to a .BSP file
Print	Get print options and print the current map
Zoom%	Show current map zoom level
Zoom Bar	Change map zoom level (slider bar)
Map Tool	Call up mini map tool
Snap	Toggle Snap-to grid; select with second mouse button to change snap size
Grid	Toggle grid lines; select with second mouse button to change grid spacing
Object	Switch to Object mode (Move/Inspect)
Paint	Switch to Special/Texture mode
Structure	Switch to Structure mode
Quick Paint	Turn on Quick Paint tool for rapid assignment of line and sector attributes
Bitmap	View the bitmap fiddler
Help	Call up help or the map statistics

The map display is designed to be as easy to read as possible. One-sided lines, which are the outside of the level or a void, are shown as thick lines. This makes it easier to visualize the space. Lines with a special are shown in blue.

Object color is related to the Thing type. Monsters are orange, with more powerful monsters being a slightly lighter shade. Player objects are green. Keys are their appropriate color. Inert objects like Gore and Furniture are shown in gray. The names and colors of the display can be customized by editing the OBJECTS.DAT file. An explanation of the fields is at the top of the file.

 # Object Mode

In Object mode there are four possible actions. The actions are performed with the first or second mouse buttons from two different modes within Object mode. The different actions are:

Move Object First button, Move/Inspect mode (press T)

View/Change Object Second button, Move/Inspect mode (press T)

Insert Object First button, Insert/Delete mode (press I)

Delete Object Second button, Insert/Delete mode (press I)

To move an object, drag it with the first mouse button. To view an object and possibly change its attributes or type, click on it with the second mouse button.

To insert an object, change to Insert/Delete mode by pressing I. Select the attributes and object type to insert. Click anywhere on the map to insert the object.

To delete an object, change to Insert/Delete mode and then click on the object to be deleted with the second mouse button.

Don't forget to change back to Move/Inspect mode before attempting to move an object or you may get undesired results. You will always be in Move/Inspect mode when you go back to Object mode from one of the other major modes.

Special/Texture Mode

The display in this mode is contextual; you will see information boxes about whatever you have selected. The information displayed and the controls that are available in Special/Texture mode are shown in Table B.3.

You will usually have a sector, line, and side selected, but at times you will have only a sector or only a line selected. A selected sector is highlighted in green. A selected line is highlighted in red. A selected side is the side of the red line that faces the green sector.

Make a selection by clicking on the map. If you click in a sector away from any lines, you will select just the sector. If you select a line from the outside of the sectors, you will select only the line. Clicking near a line on the side of it that faces a sector selects that sector, line, and side.

If the line you are clicking on has an opposite side, you can select it with the second mouse button in the same manner you would select its first side. In the case of a

one-sided line, you can select the sector that line faces while clicking on the outside. You can toggle back and forth between the two sides of a two-sided line in this way. You should experiment in the editor with an existing level, clicking with both mouse buttons to get a feel for how this works.

TABLE B.3 Controls and Information Displayed in Special/Texture Mode

Name	Meaning
INFORMATION FOR THE CURRENT SECTOR	
C_Height	Height of the ceiling (upper blue box)
F_Height	Height of the floor (lower blue box)
C_Texture	Texture of the ceiling; name is shown in white on the upper texture box in the upper-left corner of the display.
F_Texture	Texture of the floor
Brightness	Light level of the sector (white box)
Sector Special	Special attribute of this sector, if any (left green box)
Sector Tag	Tag of this sector to associate with a line, if any (right green box)
Total Height	Total distance between the floor and ceiling of this room (must not be negative)
ADDITIONAL CONTROLS ON THE CURRENT SECTOR INFORMATION BOX	
Texture List	Contains flats from current palette
Texture Box	Displays appearance of current flat choice; drag this texture and drop it on the floor or ceiling to assign a new texture

TABLE B.3	Continued
Name	**Meaning**
Palette Icon	Displays the Floor/Ceiling texture palette editor
Special	Shows the current special value and allows easy selection of a different one
Get Tag	Assigns the next available (unused) tag number to this sector
Find Tag	Highlights any line with the same tag value

INFORMATION FOR THE CURRENT LINE

Name	Meaning
Line Attributes	Select the attributes for this line
Line Special	Special attribute of this line, if any (left red box)
Line Tag	Tag of this line to associate it with a sector, if any (right red box)

ADDITIONAL CONTROLS ON THE CURRENT LINE INFORMATION BOX

Name	Meaning
Special	Shows the current special value and allows easy selection of a different one
Get Tag	Assigns the next available (unused) tag number to this line
Find Tag	Highlights any sector with the same tag value

INFORMATION FOR THE CURRENT SIDE

Name	Meaning
Line Width	The total width of this line—used for determining texture size and offset (number to right of Palette icon)
Texture Names	The textures assigned to the upper, lower, and normal of the side (white boxes)

(Continues)

TABLE B.3	Continued
Name	**Meaning**
X and Y offsets	The amount by which to shift the texture within the wall space (gray boxes)

ADDITIONAL CONTROLS ON THE CURRENT SIDE INFORMATION BOX

Palette Icon	Displays the Wall Textures palette editor for palette editing or visual texture picking
Texture List	The wall textures from the current palette
Use	Assigns currently displayed texture from the Texture List to this part of the side, or displays hidden texture name
	Assign a blank texture to this part of the side

Working with Textures

There are hundreds of textures available in Doom. To make working with this large number of textures manageable, the editor works with texture palettes.

A texture palette is simply a list of texture names. Each palette file contains a group of wall and flat textures. Palettes are created, loaded, and managed with the palette editors.

The Flats palette editor is very simple to use. The textures are shown to you as you scroll through their names (see Figure B.1). When you want to add a texture to the palette you are creating or editing, you drag its name from the list box at the left into the list at the right.

FIGURE B.1

The Flats palette.

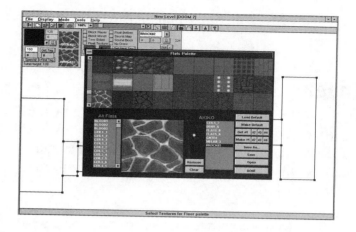

In order for you to use a given texture, it must first be added to the current palette, or be part of a palette that you switch to. You can create as many palettes as you want to, containing any textures. They may be saved to any name you see fit.

The Wall Texture palette is a little more complex, because the textures themselves are (Figure B.2). When you select a texture from the list, you see it drawn onto the palette box. Notice how it appears in sections. These sections are the patches. Each texture may be made of one or more textures; some textures in Doom are made of as many as 40 patches.

FIGURE B.2

The Wall Texture

palette.

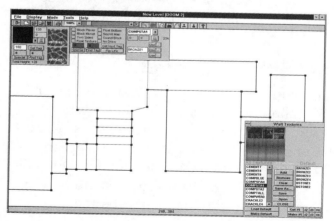

To add the displayed texture to the palette, click on the Add button.

Managing Palettes

When the editor starts up, it will load a palette by the name of DEFAULT. You can change the default palette from the palette editor by pressing the Make Default button; this will simply save the current palette to the name DEFAULT.

The best way to work with textures is to determine what textures you want to use on the level you are currently working on, and then create a few palettes containing all the textures you will need. Create up to four palettes and save them under names that will help you remember what the textures are for. For example, you might create DOORS, MARBLE, STONE, and METAL.

You then can assign each one to one of the four palette slots. This is done by having a palette loaded and pressing the appropriate Make button. Load the DOORS palette and press Make #1, then load MARBLE and press Make #2, and so on. When you return to the editor, you can switch between these four lists of textures by pressing Ctrl+1, 2, 3, or 4. The settings for these palettes will be remembered from session to session.

Picking Single Textures

The Wall Textures palette editor is very versatile. In addition to allowing you to modify your palette list, you can also use it to pick individual textures. When you click on a texture in the palette list, it appears ready for use in the list on the SideDef information display. You can then assign the texture you are viewing to the current line by pressing the Use button.

Quick Paint

The Quick Paint tool allows you to rapidly modify the attributes of lines, sides, and sectors. To use the Quick Paint tool, you must first be in Special/Texture mode and set the attributes you want to paint with.

Pick a line, side, and/or texture and assign the attributes you want to set. Select the Quick Paint tool with the button on the toolbar. A list of attribute types appears, and you can select which items you intend to change. Now you can assign those attributes to any line, side, or sector by clicking on the map.

This is a very powerful tool and can be dangerous if used indiscriminately so you may want to save the level first. Be very careful when choosing what attributes to modify. In particular, pay attention to line attributes.

Structure Mode

The display in this mode is as clean as possible. Only lines and vertexes are displayed on the screen, and the tools are simple but powerful.

Drawing Tools

There are two main tools used in Structure mode: the Vertex tool and the Sector tool. The Vertex tool allows you to move vertexes and insert new vertexes. Vertexes are moved simply by dragging them. New vertexes are inserted on lines by clicking on them with the second mouse button. The line will break and snap-to where you clicked the mouse.

The Vertex tool can also be used to delete lines. To delete a line, drag the vertex at one end of the line until it is over the vertex at the other end of the line. The vertexes will join and the line will be removed.

The Sector tool is used to draw new sectors and voids, and to delete sectors.

To draw a new sector, select the Sector tool and drag out a box. If you draw the new sector so that it lies on top of or nearly on top of an adjacent sector, the editor will try to join the sectors. In order for this to work properly, the line of the new sector that is next to the adjacent (older) sector must be equal to or shorter than the existing sector side. This will become clear after you use the tool a few times.

To delete a sector, highlight it (green) and then press D. If you are deleting a sector within a sector, you will be left with a void. (Voids are spaces within sectors, and can *only* be created within sectors; they are drawn using the second mouse button.) If you decide to retain the void, be certain to clear any leftover two-sided line attributes. To remove the void, use the Vertex tool to drag lines together. You will eventually have one line; drag the ends of the line together until you have only a vertex. The void is now gone.

The two secondary tools used in Structure mode are the AutoStruct tool and the Ruler. The AutoStruct tool is used in much the same way as the Sector tool. To change the settings of the AutoStruct tool, select its icon with the second mouse button.

File Management

When you save a level, it is written to a .BSP file. This file contains all the level data minus the part generated by the BSP program. The file is then processed by a BSP program and copied to a file with the extension .WAD.

The editor has a safety feature to avoid overwriting a file previously saved under the same name. When the editor saves a .BSP file, it first looks for a file by the same name with the .WAD extension. If it finds it, it copies that .WAD to a file with the extension .X1. If there is already a file with the name .X1, it is renamed as .X2, .X2 is renamed to .X3, and so on up to .X9.

This means you have up to nine backup copies of the level you are working on. To load the .X files from within the editor, in the file dialog choose Auto Backup for the type of file; files with .X? extensions will be shown.

FIGURE B.3

File save

protection.

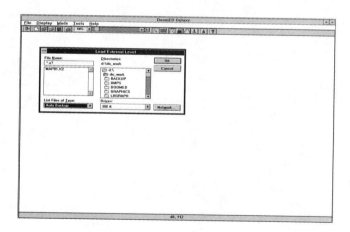

If you edit an .X file and then save it by the same name, the editor will remember that you were editing a backup file and will not create additional backups (Figure B.3). This serves to protect you from losing your good version of a level.

You should occasionally clear out the extra .X files. You can remove all of them with the command:

```
del *.X?
```

To delete only the oldest ones, specify *.X9 or *.X8 and *.X9 in your command.

WAD Description File

As you can imagine, with all the people who are creating new Doom levels, there is quite a dizzying array of new ones. When it first became possible to edit Doom levels, several dozen files called "E1M1.ZIP" showed up on the networks. Each of them was different, but there was no convention for naming or keeping these levels straight.

It is recommended that you name WADs you intend to distribute according to a formula. Use your initials and then up to three letters or numbers. This keeps the file-name short so that brain-dead online services that only allow six-character filenames won't rename your file and cause confusion.

If you are going to distribute a WAD, *please fill out a wad_auth.txt file and include it.* It really helps users keep the heaps of WADs straight, and someone might be genuinely interested in knowing more about your level before or after getting ground up by it. You should save the completed file with the same name as your WAD but with the TXT extension. It is also wise to include a file called FILE_ID.DIZ containing a one paragraph description of your level for use in BBS directory listings.

You will find this file on the enclosed disk as WAD_AUTH.TXT. The following should give you a general idea of how to fill it out:

```
Title  : Kill em all
Filename: xxxnnn.WAD
Author  : Your name here
Email Address   : me@service.com
Misc. Author Info       : Your extra info here
Description     : Set the mood here.
Additional Credits to : My spouse for putting up
          with me playing Doom all the time.
```

* Play Information *

Episode and Level #   : ExMx (,ExMx,MAPxx...)
Single Player   : Yes/No
Cooperative 2-4 Player : Yes/No
DeathMatch 2-4 Player   : Yes/No
Difficulty Settings   : Yes/Not implemented
New Sounds   : Yes/No
New Graphics   : Yes/No
New Music   : Yes/No
Demos Replaced   : None/1/2/3/All

* Construction *
Base   : New level from scratch/Modified
           ExMx/xxx.WAD
Editor(s) used : Renegade Graphics DoomED
                   Deluxe
Known Bugs   :

* Copyright / Permissions *
Authors *(MAY/may NOT)* use this level as a base
to build additionallevels.

(One of the following three options)
You MAY distribute this WAD, provided you
include this file, with
no modifications. You may distribute this file
in any electronic
format (BBS, Diskette, CD, etc) as long as you
include this file
intact.

You MAY NOT distribute this WAD file in any format.

You may do whatever you want with this file.

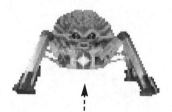

APPENDIX C

```
* Where to get this WAD *
FTP sites:
BBS numbers:
Other:
 Place any additional information you want to
include here.
```

Using the Doom Sound, Music, and Graphics Managers Included on the CD-ROM

On the CD you will find a variety of utilities for manipulating and changing the sound, music, and graphics of Doom. These programs are sometimes inaccurately referred to as editors—what they really are is managers for importing and exporting sound resources created with other programs.

All sound- and music-related utilities on the CD are in the UTIL directory beneath the SOUND directory and have documentation on disk, the graphics utilities are in the GRAPHICS directory. Here is a brief overview of these utilities:

DMAUD Performs conversion between several audio file formats; will import sounds from and export them to WAD files

MIDI2MUS Not actually related to Doom, but a convenient utility because it converts the popular MIDI or MID format of music files into MUS files which can then be imported into Doom

NWT New Wad Tool, imports and exports a wide range of resources to and from WAD files

DMGRAPH Imports graphics from and exports graphics to WADs, including conversion of GIF files

 # Handling Graphics

The Doom palette is limited to 256 colors at any one time, and a limited range of shades for any one color. Careful use of color is essential to attractive textures and sprites. At the high levels of magnification that occur when a player is near a wall or object, individual pixels are highly visible. Because of this, dithering pixels of multiple colors to achieve another color is not recommended. What looks good on a small picture on your screen may look very bad close up.

Work at the highest level of magnification you find comfortable. This will help you see more clearly how the graphic will look in the game.

The Color Palette

Colors used in graphics you create that are not exact matches of colors in the Doom palette will be changed to the closest matching color when the graphic is inserted into a WAD by a utility such as DMGRAPH. It is highly recommended that you only use colors from the Doom palette when creating graphics; otherwise your new graphics will look quite different when they are imported.

To make it easier for you to match the Doom palette, there is a BMP on the CD in the GRAPHICS directory called DOOMPAL.BMP. This is simply a block of colors containing the full Doom palette. Load this file and use it to pick colors from or generate a palette for the paint program you use.

Open Spaces

Sprites and some texture patches have open space in them. Within the graphic format used by Doom, the spaces are integral to the data. The graphic importing utilities need a method to recognize where you want blank space to be, since there is no way to represent this with normal graphic editors. The method that is used by DMGRAPH and other utilities is to treat any cyan color pixels as blank space.

Cyan has an RGB value of 0, 255, 255. By entering these specific values in the color picker or palette of

your graphics editing program (such as Corel Photo-Paint or HiJaak 3), you can use cyan to indicate blank spaces. If you do not know how to create a color from a specific RGB value in the graphic editor you are using, refer to its documentation.

 # Handling Music

Any music you have to use or that you create will most likely be in the MIDI file format. Music must be converted from the MID format to the MUS format before it can be imported into a WAD file. To do this, simply use the command:

```
MIDI2MUS file.MID
```

 # Handling Sound

New sounds and music should usually be placed into an external WAD file by themselves. This gives you, and anyone using your work, the option of using them with the original Doom levels or with external WADs.

Capturing Good Sounds

The quality of the sound you use is as important as what the sound is.

No guidelines can really be given for what sounds to use. If you think a sound is cool or funny, it's your prerogative to use it. Some people might consider a particular sound to be in bad taste. Of course this might be what you are going for, but you should include a warning to help people avoid being embarrassed or offended.

Always remember that while you may capture sounds for your own use off of CDs and other source material that you own, you cannot distribute those sounds for use by anyone else. Never distribute samples from copyrighted material.

How to Capture It

The quality of sound is important. If you are capturing directly from a tape or CD source, the quality is beyond your control. If you are generating and recording the sound yourself, you have some degree of control over the sound quality.

If you are capturing sound with a microphone and digitizing directly with the sound board in your computer, you must take steps to minimize background noise such as from the computer fan. Try to get the microphone as far from the computer as possible, or even into another room. You will get the best sound quality when there are a lot of soft surfaces around to absorb noise. A bedroom will usually make do as a sound studio.

If you have never used your sound board to capture sound before, read through the documentation that came with it. Nearly all sound cards come with some sort of sound capture software, usually Windows based. Remember that the final quality of the sounds in Doom is always 11,025 samples per second; working at a much higher sample rate will waste storage space and will not have any effect on the final sound.

APPENDIX D

Effects

Your samples will usually sound better if they are given some depth through the use of reverb or a slight echo. Without the use of this type of mixing, sounds will seem flat. This is especially true of environmental sounds such as the sound of a door closing.

See the documentation for the sound capture software you have with your sound card to see if it offers an "Add Echo" feature. Experiment with different amounts of echo until you find a mixture you are happy with.

Other techniques to try:

- Mix multiple copies of the same sound together for an overlapped effect.
- Cut the sample in half and use a small amount of echo on the first part and a larger echo on the latter part, then re-join them.

Index